Neighborhood Hawks

Neighborhood Hawks

A Year Following Wild Birds

JOHN LANE

The University of Georgia Press ⚹ *Athens*

A Wormsloe
FOUNDATION
nature book

© 2019 by the University of Georgia Press
Athens, Georgia 30602
www.ugapress.org
All rights reserved
Designed by Erin Kirk New
Set in 10 on 14 Warnock Pro
Printed and bound by Thomson-Shore
The paper in this book meets the guidelines for
permanence and durability of the Committee on
Production Guidelines for Book Longevity of the
Council on Library Resources.

Most University of Georgia Press titles are
available from popular e-book vendors.

Printed in the United States of America
19   20   21   22   23   C   5   4   3   2   1

Library of Congress Cataloging-in-Publication Data

Names: Lane, John, 1954– author.
Title: Neighborhood hawks : a year following wild birds /
    John Lane.
Description: Athens : The University of Georgia Press,
    [2019]
Identifiers: LCCN 2018034309 | ISBN 9780820354934
    (paperback : alk. paper)
Subjects: LCSH: Red-shouldered hawk—South Carolina.
    | Lane, John, 1954– —Diaries. | Human-animal
    relationships—South Carolina.
Classification: LCC QL696.F32 L332 2019 |
    DDC 598.9/44—dc23 LC record available at
    https://lccn.loc.gov/2018034309

For Barry Lopez

Friend & Mentor

"The interior of woods seems . . . the fittest haunts of the
Red-shouldered Hawk. He sails through them a few yards above
the ground, and suddenly alights on a low branch of a tree,
or a dead stump, from which he silently watches."
    —JOHN JAMES AUDUBON

"the bright cold hawks—
    you've made friends with them now—"
        —ROBINSON JEFFERS

Contents

The Beaver Ponds

Swamp

LAWSON'S FORK

THE HOME
TERRITORY

Neighborhood Hawks

Beginnings

I first noticed our neighborhood hawks nesting in an immense red oak in our side woods fifteen years ago, soon after Betsy and I built our house here. I thought the birds were red-tailed hawks, ubiquitous to southern American uplands, until I got a good look and saw clearly the brown and white bands on the wings and tail, the red shoulders, and the speckled cinnamon underparts shining in the sun. A quick glance at my Peterson's guide identified them as red-shouldered hawks, preferring "swamps" and "damp woodlands" to the red-tails' "open country, woodlands, and roadsides." So right away, even though we were new to the neighborhood, I found common ground and purpose with these river rats of the hawk clan, birds like me with a strong preference for nearby watery realms.

I assumed the nest failed. I found a number of broken eggs—ovate, pale blue, blotched with brownish red—below the tree and in the suburban road beside it. Raccoon? Negligence by the parent hawks? I'll never know. The next year the hawks moved their nest across the street to another big red oak in a neighbor's backyard. The neighbor soon complained about the hawks. He accused them of dive-bombing his car and made a joke about shooting them. I reminded him about the $10,000 fine for each bird. The neighbor is long departed, the house foreclosed on in the Great Recession of 2008, but the birds made it through, invested as they are in a vast stock market that seems to offer them a small but consistent return, season to season.

The birds, or later generations of the birds, remain. My ornithologist friends are quick to remind me that telling individual birds apart is almost impossible unless they are banded or have some distinguishing characteristic, such as an oddness of color. But ever since that first spring living here, I have appreciated the red-shouldered hawks and marked their presence from time to time, noisy neighbors if there ever were.

Sometimes I couldn't help but take deeper notice though—like the day years ago when one dropped at my wife's feet, grabbed a foot-long northern brown snake, and flew away; or the time I came home early one afternoon from teaching and found a hawk sitting on the back of the glider on our side porch because I'd neglected to close the screened door.

We live in a South Carolina piedmont creek valley shaped like an old-fashioned breadboard, the opposite low rims (the ridges) running east and west. The creek is the axis of the valley flowing south/southeast. The waterway splits the landscape down the middle, the upper end just above town and the lower reaching all the way past a mill village below us built on a large shoals. At the mill village the creek takes on the personality of a mountain stream racing through the lower valley before its confluence with a larger river. The creek down there has steeper slopes covered with mountain laurel and dog hobble where the slope faces north. The stream is rocky in many places and precipitous enough to be called rapids. Our neighborhood consists of one fishhook of a street along the edge of the floodplain, ending in a cul-de-sac. There are ten houses, each with a backyard opening out on woods. The houses to the south, like ours, have the creek running along the lots' back edge, and a large, wild floodplain runs east and west beyond that.

Before we built our house, the hawks probably flew through our patch of hardwoods with abandon. Then we plopped this human impediment down in their paths and occasionally our dreams and the realities of the hawks collide. From the yard, I look back at the house and its broad forehead opens into the blue sky speckled with white puffy clouds. Any hawk would see escape there and fly into our windows. I have witnessed it twice. I want to believe it's mostly the young and foolish who take glass for sky. I want to believe adults can see their way around such traps.

Bird hazard or not, this house is an object of our love. We built it out of mutual dreams. We had it constructed based on our sense of a loving space. It's open and airy. We live in it. We, like the hawks, are mated for the duration. This is our home territory and my affection in particular often flows outward, past the windows and walls of this human habitation. Love for a landscape is often colored by contact, and the piedmont woods are something I know well. I grew up here, and even the other places I've lived—in Vermont, the Sea Islands, the Blue Ridge, the Puget Sound—always opened up extreme cases of homesickness for the piedmont within me. It took me, like Odysseus, ten years to return and plant my oar, but I finally did in the late 1980s. It's now late in the second decade of the 2000s and I've been back around awhile, and somehow, as hard as it is to believe, we've been in this house for a decade and a half.

What I always wanted most once I returned was to have a place to walk in the woods, but I have settled peacefully for walking in the neighborhood. The owners of the large tracts behind us (the bottoms up- and downstream) hunt, or, lease the land for others to hunt, so walking there is often technically off-limits. Because of that, I stick mostly to the roads and walking daily a short stretch of trail behind our house. Five or six times a year the creek floods and fills the bottoms, and up at the house I want to believe I attend to the river in all its moods, so I listen like a supplicant to the muddy water shushing through the trees and flattening the weeds.

Trash washes in, for this is an urban creek. Oddly enough, the primary items I find besides plastic drink bottles are balls of all sizes, including tiny pink ones from a McDonald's playground four miles upstream. Flood-time is one of the periods when the land turns musical. The other is when drifts of birds move in to feed.

I would not call myself a birdwatcher, though daily I do watch birds. I'm competent with a dozen wading birds and ducks, the local hawks, the occasional osprey and bald eagle, three common woodpeckers, and all the foraging birds at the bird feeder—cardinals, titmice, nuthatches, Carolina wrens, chickadees. That leaves me a few hundred short on the four hundred and twenty-seven species of the avifauna of South Carolina, but I have become pretty good with a field guide and my iPhone's iBird Pro. I learn the warblers every spring when they move through, and then I forget them by the time they return in the fall.

I've written about many of the animals in the woods around us—turtles, snakes, and the coyotes that howl across the flood plain—but writing about these resident, nonmigratory red-shouldered hawks occurred to me only after I had discovered J. A. Baker's *The Peregrine*. Baker proved an unlikely but inspiring literary mentor—introverted, arthritic, and nearsighted—with a day job for decades as a clerk for the British Automobile Association, though he never drove. Writing in Essex an ocean away and dead now thirty years, Baker had published his intense prose poem about following migrating falcons on the English coast in 1967. Over the course of one mythical year he tracks the birds wherever he finds them. *The Peregrine* won one major British literary prize, then went out of print for more than thirty years. But the book survived literary extinction and resurfaced in a reprint by *New York Review of Books* in 2005.

The text of *The Peregrine* is as dense and contagious as any I've ever encountered. The book swallowed me. The prose is so poetic and kinetic at times that I simply had to stop reading and breathe. Once discovered, I consumed the first part of *The Peregrine* in a fury; I took notes in the margins, highlighting Baker's explosive verbs—ripple, sputter, sweep, scold, cackle—tracking the one he calls "the watcher" and the watcher's shamanic efforts to leave human form and become a hunting falcon.

In *The Peregrine* the watcher gives advice as to how to be accepted by a raptor, what to wear and how to walk, for Baker believed that his book would be a guide for passing over into the realm of the birds for anyone willing to pay the price—in his case ten years watching on the Essex sea flats. He says hawk hunting made his vision sharper. J. A. Baker died in 1987 at age sixty-one, from cancer brought on by complications from the drugs used to treat his severe arthritis, and I read his book the year I turned sixty-one. I am lucky. Most of my pain so far comes from aging—creaky knees and aching hips. My eyesight is still good.

But another difference between Baker's watcher and me is that the watcher believes he is witnessing the last act on a set stage. He thinks that because of pesticides the peregrine falcons would not survive very long. He talks about the beauty of the peregrines, and the wonder of the land they live in, as if his book is an elegy to a vanishing species. Baker was wrong. Since Baker wrote in the early 1960s, thanks to Rachel Carson and *Silent Spring* and the banning of DDT, peregrines have made a comeback everywhere and even flourish in urban places he would have never imagined, cities such as London and New York. Other hawks have prospered in the last few decades as well—red-tails, red-shoulders, Cooper's—though there are still threats maybe as serious as DDT once was, such as habitat loss, land fragmentation, climate change, wind farms, poisoning, electrocution, raptor persecution, and disease. Driving around here it's not unusual to see a half dozen hawks in one day. They survive in the city, the country, the suburbs. The Cornell Lab's website, called All About Birds, lists all the common hawks of the southern piedmont as of "low" or "least" concern in conservation status.

In spite of our differences I was drawn into *The Peregrine* by its sheer verve as literary text, but Baker's words had also acted as a set of binoculars, focusing for me my own experience in this particular place. Baker's elsewhere became my home ground, and his birds transmogrified into my neighborhood hawks. I knew from when I first started reading that, though we shared a quest through time, I was different from Baker. I wasn't as obsessed or focused as the Essex literary mystic or his watcher. Early on in *The Peregrine*, the watcher says that people native to the clay of his beloved Essex coast are "surly and slow to burn, morose and smoldering as alder wood, laconic, heavy as the land itself." This is not me. Though I am native to this southern American piedmont clay, I am much more like the beagles we prefer as pets—with an inclination toward pursuit, nose to ground, or in the case of this project, eyes and ears to the trees. When I burn, it is with the intensity of yellow poplar. It's a hot flame but needs to be fed often. My engagement was leading me somewhere—into an adventure of watching and knowing—but I didn't know exactly where. That's when I made a vow that for one year I would follow the neighborhood hawks wherever they took me. If I heard or saw them in the yard, I would track them as far as they went. So I disappeared inside Baker's text as thousands of other readers had, but then did what I know of no one else doing, at least in the United States—I crawled back out, noticed the hawks in my own neighborhood in a different way, and began to write my own way into this place.

I know this is a congested time to write about hawks because of Helen McDonald's *H Is for Hawk*, which was recently on best-seller lists. Of course, there are many differences between what I expected from the hawks in my neighborhood and what McDonald expected from hers. In McDonald's book the bird in question is a goshawk, purchased, trained, and cared for; besides the animal narrative, McDonald marbles her own story with grief over the death of her father, and she leans heavily on several literary models to highlight hidden lives. I liked the information about the hawk, but McDonald's plotline is what pulled me along and what made this book a best seller in England and America. The protagonist fights depression about her father's death. She learns to care for a hawk. She unearths the connections between birds and people and she finds hope in such relationships. She recovers. But obviously, McDonald's book is only peripherally about hawks. *H* could also stand for human, and all the ways we humans are distracted from the natural world.

In *H Is for Hawk* McDonald references Baker's *The Peregrine* too, but portrays Baker's watcher as having little hope, and calls his book a eulogy about annihilation. I'm glad I started reading Baker before I read McDonald. Baker allowed me to find my own way into the world of birds of prey and humans and form my own conclusions.

But after only sixty-eight pages of *The Peregrine* I stalled, like a beagle that has lost the scent. I think what suspended my reading was Baker's accounts of the deaths of birds, prey of the peregrines. I staggered under the weight of all the death. From the start Baker's hunting journal depicts darkness and dizzying motion. There seems to be a dead bird on every page. The first peregrine he describes soars and drifts among plumes of gulls and plovers. In ten seasons following the Essex peregrines, Baker recorded 619 kills, so his quest yielded what he seems to have desired, a macabre grail.

I finally finished *The Peregrine* months later on a trip to Newfoundland. Every time my wife and I saw a gathering of sea birds on the Newfoundland coast I *imagined* Baker's birds falling like death from above, because he had described the birds falling with such precision. But then, as if I had conjured it, I finally encountered a peregrine and watched it stoop, drop rapidly, like a Stuka bomber over a far north blue crinoline bay. The dive was breathtaking. In a head-first, tucked plummet, through what seemed half the sky, the falcon caught up with the sea bird it was pursuing and used some hidden slab of air to pivot—but then somehow the gull it chased made the right lifesaving move and wiggled out of death's crosshairs and fled. Though I had imagined a kill, instead I tracked the falcon back to the rocky cliffs, where it disappeared among the ledges of ancient granite. I assumed it was tending a nest.

So I followed the neighborhood hawks for a year. I kept a journal. I sat on our screened porch and listened, observing their constant comings and goings. I walked our one street in and out of the neighborhood and looked up into the wooded lots above and down into the floodplain below. At first, as an incentive to keep me hunting, I tried to find some remnants of an old nest in the forks of the largest oaks. A nest seemed a good place to start, for I knew that these birds often build in the same tree—or one nearby—for generations. I did not collect my observations for ten years like Baker, but I did record what I saw, heard, and thought for a full year, from late June to late June. I tracked these hawks as they moved among us. I did not know when I embarked if anything notable would come of it. Baker claimed to be trying to preserve some unity that, as he put it, binds together bird, watcher, and place. That is close to what I set out to do as well. In my year following the hawks, I often felt like a visitor in someone else's living room, as if I had crossed a threshold and needed to ask permission of the birds to sit down and converse. Watching them for a year was like shaking hands at a door.

Though the peregrines did not vanish from the earth, as Baker expected, fifty years after his book was published it's still easy to find what he called "the human taint" in our suburb (screaming weed eaters, barking dogs, the wail of leaf blowers, lawn mowers, and the manic acceleration of teenage drivers with hormones to stanch, punctuated by UPS trucks with delivery quotas to meet) and to veer, like Baker, toward misanthropy. But I find it comforting to walk our suburban streets and track the human activity, and then look into the wild, adjacent floodplain off to one side and note natural attractions, such as the dark silent potholes of standing rain in the wetlands, and then glance up the other direction into the clipped lawns of our neighbors and admire the calm faces of their midcentury moderns staring toward the street. It was Baker's quest to follow the peregrines in Essex, and his desire passed over into a book. I learned, if I listened long enough, that I would always see or hear the wild hawks below.

The Almanac

since feeling is first / who pays any attention / to the syntax of things.
—E. E. CUMMINGS

Summer

30 June. Our drought deepens weekly, persistent since March. The air smells parched. The privet is dead in the bottoms. I water the yard plants every other day. Gray squirrels have started to strip the coleus. Returning from the farmers market yesterday, I dropped a peach in the driveway. Something found it overnight, ate half, and then abandoned what remained in the defeated ferns. The deer eat yard plants they haven't touched in fourteen years. This morning for the first time I heard the whirring of the cicadas, like the motor of summer finally turned over. First they buzzed to my left, then to the right, strung together by the constant murmuring of a Carolina wren between. As morning hinges into afternoon, following a quick thunderstorm, a hawk bathes in a rain puddle on asphalt at the subdivision front gate.

1 July. These red-shouldered hawks are the size of a quart-sized carton of milk, with a long tail and broad wings almost checkerboarded with white and brown, set against their reddish, compact bodies. In size they are halfway between a sparrow hawk and a red-tailed hawk, both birds I have seen in the neighborhood.

The field guides say of telling the sexes apart, "forget it." But one of our birds is larger, sounds more hoarse than the other. Is that a way to tell them apart? Or is it that both birds get hoarse because they call so much? One of our neighbors down the street says she hates these birds because of their calling. She has a free-ranging Yorkie and lives in fear "those damn hawks" will snatch the little dog. The birds *are* vocal;

the various sounds they make have been described as "peep-ing" in nestlings, trending into "chirps" as they grow older. There are six recognized calls among the adults and I've heard them all: the common *kee-aah*, with the accent on the first syllable, a stretched-out second syllable with a down-ward bounce, sometimes repeated a dozen times; *kee-wee*, a variation on the first; *kip*, used in alarm; *kee-yip*, heard when they are excited; *kee-ann-errr*, when adults are courting; and finally the soft and brief *kee*, used sometimes by the female when brooding. Some guides refer to the birds' courtship cries as wild songs. If they are singers, then they are making music all the time. We live within the home range of the red-shouldered hawks, and their vocalizations are as regular as our favorite radio station. Their bird cries echo through the nearby wooded spaces throughout the daylight hours. Sound becomes destiny.

3 July. Cool morning air. A hawk calls to the east. Kee-yer, kee-yer, kee-yer, the vocalization is extraverted and edgy, a calling card, mixed (as they are mixed in) with the mechanical drone of a passing plane, the whistle of titmice at the feeding tube, cardinals canvasing, a nervous Carolina wren, and a nuthatch in the yaupon holly. Through it all, a hawk's cry, rasping the sky like a file.

4 July. One of the hawks swoops from a sentinel perch on the low branch of a box elder, then slashes across the suburb entrance in front of my moving truck. It cruises in low just as I turn the corner and then squats on the ground in the grass next to the kudzu trimline. The bird sits there with wings hooded, as if some prey is hidden underneath. I slow and then stop the truck. The hawk hops once on the grass, squares up, shows me the warm, burnished chest bars of its vestments, looks at me straight on, and then bolts toward the windscreen. At the last moment it jacks both buteo wings into blunt scissor blades and veers away. Then the hawk brakes low to land on the same limb it had originally taken off from. When I accelerate again the hawk rouses its feathers like a dismissal before settling hard on the limb and picking up each yellow leg, one by one.

Later in the afternoon I hear not one but two red-shouldereds together, kee-youing in the wooded vacant lots to the north. The temperature has reached ninety-five. They are either bickering or belaboring a contested point, like the habituated husband and wife they are. Their voices are stringent, metallic, looped through the suburban trees like pulled wire. They call a hundred times.

5 July. Where are their habitual neighborhood perches? Only long and sustained attention will reveal these. I watch the sky, but these hawks are rarely soaring. So instead I watch the ground for patches bleached white with hawk void. I'm hoping that the sites of their perches will help me find their nest later in the year.

As I think about hawks and humans, I consider the term "neighbor." It's a slippery word, its origins submerged in Old English, *neah*, or "near," combined with *gebur*, or "dweller." "Near dwellers." Neighbors—you expect things from them. It's one of the building-block relationships of human community. Humans have had neighbors since the dawn of our species. Even caves must have been a sense of ordered space.

"Neighborhood" adds in another ancient etymological element, that of the suffix "-hood," a little more recent, from the Middle English, and suggesting "a condition, a state, a nature," opening up all sorts of room in the mind of a poet for metaphoric collision of other species in a place.

Searching for differing and elastic meanings of "neighbor" and "neighborhood," in my reading I discovered commensalism, the biological idea that individuals of different species can have a relationship in which one species obtains food or other benefits without either harming or benefiting the other. It's easy to see the commensal birds benefiting from my bird feeder. But it's hard—and maybe downright impossible—to know for sure what food or commensal benefits a hawk gets from intersecting with my backyard.

But maybe these neighborhood hawks can be considered "commensal" with us humans. Do I receive commensal benefits from them? How about the daily material for my observations and speculations?

7 July. I stare out at the floodplain as if it's a riddle that can be solved. Where are the hawks? Do they joust with today's wind? Red-shouldered hawks live mostly in the cluttered world of the forest understory. Or at least the woods look cluttered to these human eyes. The hawks tilt and careen through low limbs and brush jumbles. They dive and slice through the parallel planes of wood, foliage, and air. The woodland patterns are there to be exploited—the predictable spread of oak and popular limb swirls, the shapes imprinted on closed space the hawks navigate.

What a hawk sees is dense piedmont forest in every direction, and from above. Our house is hidden, April to November, under parasols of broad photosynthesizing leaves. The pinching edge of these remaining woods enclose our subdivision. These hawks, unlike Baker's peregrines, don't migrate. They stay around and learn the familiar warrens of our wooded yard; they tilt through intimate suburban forests. They settle down on predictable parallel perches. They live in a world of endless seasonal change and project the steady calculation of a predator out to the edges of their home ranges.

8 July. One of the hawks is a silhouette against the cerulean dawn sky washed clean by last night's storms. It's a perfect cross, what the field guide describes as "the buteo shape (broad, rounded wings; short tail)," but the glimpse lasts only five seconds. The hawk passes with such assurance, close enough for clarity. Then it's over the bottoms along the creek, calling among the morning crows.

Then through the oaks another hawk rises up and lands on a large oak, the first hawk still calling near the creek. Farther down in the branches the titmice bicker. Above, the hawks string the sharper, longer notes of their vocation against the rising day.

9 July. I should get off this glider and go look for the source of the hawk calls before the heat rises. But there are so many birds in the yard's soundscape that are not hawks—a wild turkey clucking to the south in the bottoms, cardinals in almost every cardinal direction, titmice at the feeder, crows offended by something north of here. Suddenly, breaking from the southern woods, a hawk crosses low over the house and sutures the morning's tapestry again like a needle.

There are four new arrivals in the yard. These crows don't yet know I am watching. Like four black holes appearing in the garden, they strut back and forth, then dip, one by one, in the birdbath, their bills slightly ajar in the heat.

10 July. When is chick time? April? May? If they have chicks next year, I want to see them fledge and fly. If I find the nest.

11 July. The heat is the still story. It lays thick on the woodlands like a tin sheet. Scalded weeds shrivel in the paths. The oak leaf hydrangeas droop. A defeated gray squirrel stretches out prone, spread-eagle on the deck boards in a hood of shade. How does such dry and hot weather (weeks now without significant rain) affect the resident hawks, the successful denizens of wet bottomlands since the Oligocene?

As if to answer my question, at high noon one of the two hawks flies through the branches lower in the bottoms—noisy, fretful, but by no means defeated by the drought.

I grab my binoculars and take off down the dry trail into the woods in the general direction the hawk disappeared. I wander from shade spot to shade spot. Down on the creek the current has dwindled to a whisper, but soon the shadows fling a kingfisher downstream, arrowing past with surprising, harrowing laughter, wings folded, another adapted predator of this creek valley.

I hear a hawk a long way off, somewhere north of the cul-de-sac. Then it circles back my way. I cut through the woods toward it, to pursue this conversation in the heat. As I bushwhack, it calls. It's in the northeast quadrant, beside the neighborhood's dead-end crooked finger of road. Both hawks or one? I can't tell from this distance. Then I figure out it's only one, and I follow the single bird's call up from the creek to the hardwoods in the subdivision's heart, and locate the constant caller sitting high in an alligator-barked sourwood. The red-shouldered flies as I approach, then goes silent somewhere out of sight to the east. No calls deeper in the woods. Is the nest back there? Worth the effort to pursue? Maybe on a cooler day. I head home. Thunder to the southwest. The rising heat has spawned a storm. The titmice are the only sound in the dry woods, save for a neighbor's air conditioner.

12 July. A day without hawks. The forest is stripped of some vital layer. Where do they go on a day off like this? The only birdsong is a single crow southwest of here. I know the hawks can appear at any moment, though, and burst the settled afternoon like a dart with their cries.

Today there are only hawks in my imagination. I look up into the crotch of every tall oak. There? There? There? I want to find their nest so much I create one in every tree out of squirrel nests.

13 July. One of the birds is back. Six-thirty a.m. and I hear three sharp kwees south in the floodplain. That's it. Then it's gone. Haiku birding.

14 July. I watch a yellow-billed cuckoo drop from a low branch onto a caterpillar in our cul-de-sac, carry it back to the branch, eat it, and then wipe its long beak before tiring of my vigil and flying away. At the same time, a downy woodpecker in black and white vestments works the trunk of an old dogwood in the heat.

15 July. The early birds at the feeder are at their other more silent chores—cracking seeds, flitting. For a few moments a brief false moratorium settles over the morning yard. False? Because this easy truce—the moment's silence—won't last. The sound of birds is one of the yard's constants. It is what holds it together. There is a furious intensity to suburban bird life. They live so fully.

And then, west of here, a hawk breaks the yard's brief silence with dawn's modulated cries as it moves steadily away.

19 July. Evening. A dead copperhead is on the road. I know that Baker would see it, heft the dead body, smell it even, looking carefully, then transform what is before him into language. He would describe it in this state as "natural" as life—not a state lost to sadness. I perform my unusual ritual, remove the carcass from the roadway so it does not suffer the indignity of being run over multiple times, and even say a little prayer.

24 July. We're sitting on the screened porch. I'm listening to the yard and Betsy is reading. One of the hawks calls, piercing me. Betsy notices how my attention is drawn outward. "You've become more and more connected to wild animals in the years I've known you," she says. "What does it mean when a man's heart yearns so much toward wild animals?"

26 July. I've always longed to be part of something bigger, to be a strand in John Muir's web, to vibrate as one of many plucked strings. But I've also wanted to be special, to step to Thoreau's different drummer, to be unique and outside conventional society. Is it possible to have it both ways? The web of life is bigger than any single species. Even though we humans can claim the stock market, ice cream, the Clovis point, Greek and Noh drama, and the Toyota among our species' inventions, not one of these is more important than what termites and lemurs contribute in their own lemur and termite ways. This is an easy way of saying that I don't want to be a part only of some constructed human order of things.

In childhood I was granted my wish to be a part of something weblike—I had a close extended Southern family, and I made friends easily; I wandered the woods and streams, and I felt deeply the presence of animals; at the same time, there was plenty of trauma in my family early on. I'm the child of a suicide. My father. I'm the child of an alcoholic. My mother.

I've often believed that my fierce attachment to place is connected to how much I moved in childhood. We were rootless, and now my roots are strong. Did early childhood experiences bestow a certain gravity on me? They perforated me, there's no doubt. Did my insecurities foster a sort of second nature? Even in the presence of the weblike beauty of the world, loss and abandonment were always possible.

Looking at my childhood this way it's easy to see why I'm so susceptible to realities of "Big Nature," everyday abundance and beauty, and environmental apocalypse. The idea that the world could end—through pollution, overde-velopment, overpopulation, species loss, and, most recently, climate disruption—became an intellectual stance for me. Acquiring this second nature, I anticipated loss, but loss also perpetrated and focused my interest in nature and prompts questions like, why do I spend so much time outside in the woods and wilds, and why does my heart go out to wild animals? Maybe I ask these questions because, when I was a child and I began to question, wild space created another space around the pain of home, like a bole formed around an injured twig. So I pursue these hawks for kinship, for contact, for connection. I want to feel a part of their web, which becomes clearer to me each day I pursue them.

2 August. Three cries, then silence, like a radio drifted off the station, waiting to be tuned.

4 August. In the dark night the fence of sycamores is like a screen saver of shadows on the yard's edge, and the big moon is no comfort. No hawks, but a barred owl hunts or courts on the temporal edge.

6 August. I admit to an unfounded fear when I can't hear the hawks. I worry they are dead or gone. Where do they spend their time? Right now they are quiet again, either sit-ting silently on a perch, or off in the distance. Usually their calls are so loud it's hard to imagine them out of earshot. And then there they are—calling to the south, a distant call, but a comforting call nonetheless.

Evening. We drive out of the subdivision to visit a friend and see one of the hawks on the ground at the edge of the corner floodplain. As we pass it flies up with a small snake in its talons and disappears into the trees. How do they see them? Their eyes must fire like lasers.

7 August. Odd today. The first bird as dawn bends through the eastern band of trees is a single crow. I sit on the dark screened porch and mostly it's still the crickets I hear, the background soundtrack of summer slipping toward fall.

But something has riled the single crow and now it caws over and over to the northeast—four caws. Crows live in a rising stock market. New articles about their intelligence and culture appear all the time, raising their value for us. Scientists substantiate their intelligence, and I now look to crows for a sort of assurance, finding in crow intelligence conformation that intelligence is not human but found throughout the animal kingdom. Crow intelligence is a marvel. Do they know they are the current stars of the bird world?

I hear a neighbor's dog bark and the crow's monologue goes up an octave. The caws sharpen, and each minute of the growing light more titmice and chickadees join in, their voices merging as challenge to the crows. Patches of eggshell blue are visible through the forest, lightening with each moment. The ligaments of day are stretched now by bird-song, the Carolina wren joined by others in the distance.

If I sit long enough, will I hear the hawks as well? I trust they are as much a presence in this suburban ecosystem as the frenzy at the feeder, the mechanical drone of the con-denser, the barking dog, the paper's daily delivery, and the crows.

The first cardinal of dawn appears at the feeder. It's a slate gray female feeding cracked black sunflower seeds to her fledgling. The fledgling flutters as its mother sidles up. They see me sitting on the dark porch and edge down the rail.

8 August. 6:00 p.m. Quiet all day. Then a clear hawk call from the southeast. Almost plaintive. Three times. Then three again. A little closer. Then three more from same spot. Then the mate joins in. From the west. Comes in howling. On the wing. Through the trees below me. Then both to the north. Back and forth. Now both together. Receding. Echoing as the distance swallows them. Then they are gone.

9 August. Barely dawn. The cicadas chorus the morning with their constant clicking. The ensemble rises and falls, as if led by some unseen conductor. They huddle in the dark limbs and launch nets of song down and out at the open spaces of the yard. One hawk calls. Somewhere distant and less effusive than the birds at the nearby feeder. But the hawk is on the move, north of here, and I hear it, tuned in to its waking beyond my own. Its territory is exterior and lit now, though clouds dampen the morning. Mine is enclosed by screen. Do hawks meet up and parcel the day? Do they roost together? I hope to learn these things over time but to do so I will have to leave this enclosure. Hawk time is mobile, mapped in space.

A rare recent rain has begun, rattling the leaves. Summer rain, soft and steady. In such weather where do the hawks huddle?

10 August. The backyard slopes due south, steeply down to the creek, to the vertical pillars of oaks, poplars, and sweet gum. An understory of pawpaw and Russian olive fill in between, their dull green a gauze stretched over bright patches of light leaking already from the east. The pawpaw leaves, where they push into the open space of the yard, look tropical—huge and oblong, lolling at the flimsy stem tips. The fruit ripens in August, dusky, green, banana-like, and falls to the ground where raccoons, possums, coyotes, feast, defecating the dark, almond-like seeds all through the months.

This morning the hawks work the middle range of the forest above the pawpaws. Another perch, this time on a forked hardwood, where they scan the floodplain. Only rarely do

I see them soaring. They maneuver through the branches twenty feet off the flooded turf.

Afternoon. After a rain the hawks are to the north, the direction in which the storm retreated. Rain drops from the trees, a chorus of sobs.

13 August. *—I hear you, south of me, in the flood plain, your call sharp enough to gig a frog.*

17 August. I haven't heard the hawks in days. Was it my direct address? Did I cross over some line? On my late afternoon circumambulation with the dog I hear crows canvasing in the distance, a mourning dove, and the mechanical click of a solitary cicada. On the lower trail ants crawl the fall grapes, swarming the purple nubbins burst and exhausted among the dry leaves and drifted needles. We are about a month from autumn. In the sheltered woods off the road the dog alerts me to a raccoon climbing a poplar, humping slide for slide toward the top branches. Paused, I listen to two barred owls playing vocal ping-pong—"who who cooks for you?"—separated in the woods. Territory? Exhausted summer love? An avian negotiation? Then as I walk back home I look up out of habit and see the sullen silhouette of one of the red-shouldered hawks slumped on the high perch against the marbled blue sky. I try to engage, converse in the heat. I whistle three long notes and the bird unfurls like a hinged shadow and drops into the dry air until something unseen catches its weight and hauls it upward through the wall of branches and away.

18 August. One faint cry from the west.

25 August. I have been invited to spend a few days writing at a nature center in Pennsylvania. On the way up on I-81 a red-tailed hawk flew low in front of my truck with a mouse or shrew in its beak. I expect that most of my productive time at the center will be spent walking in the woods reflecting and I won't think much about our neighborhood hawks, but when I arrived, I discovered there is a raptor center and I'm expected to write about it as one of the reflection spots all visiting writers share.

I asked the director if I could watch him feed the hawks and eagles. Later I went into the prep building with him and he pulled the day's feeding out of the refrigerator—a combination of thawed small, medium, and large rats and mice. I watched as he slipped on blue disposable gloves and used scissors to cut the carcasses into small bits for feeding, leaving the tails intact, as he said the birds really enjoy those and the heads. He may not have used the word "enjoy." That may be my projection; he was very professional and careful not to anthropomorphize, so he mostly used another term—"enrichment"—for any action or activity that might make the birds feel less captive and mimic how they live in the wild. "They seem to really like the heads," he said, matter-of-factly. He used the example of high perches to illustrate enrichment of a nonfood variety: "Raptors like to sit up high because they can see over the whole landscape. We like to give them some options."

My attention was piqued when I noticed that it was not all factory-raised rats and mice in the cups. There was a dead bird in one. "Who is that for?" I asked. "Oh, that quail? For the peregrine," he said. Then he cut the quail up into small pieces with the surgical scissors. He kept the feet on to please the peregrine. "There is little meat on these but they seem to enjoy the feet too."

I asked him if they named the birds, and he said there was a vigorous discussion under way at the center about that. Some wanted to name them and others didn't. What would it hurt? He explained that mostly they wanted to present the idea that the birds are not pets, especially when they are used as educational birds. "Naming them could interfere with that." I understood. Naming an animal at a raptor center could be a little too much like a nurse falling in love with his patient. That was a long way from simply wanting the best for them.

I watched the director work with the peregrine. The bird was skittish but performed many of its usual feeding routines, like hopping from perch to glove, then taking a small piece of the quail. The peregrine knew I was there. It would have been nice for it to know I'd read a very difficult book about its kin, but I knew that was a little too much to expect.

After the director finished his feeding of the other birds, I thanked him and stood a while longer watching the peregrine. I walked as close as I felt comfortable getting to the peregrine's cage. She was back on her highest perch, about eye-height with me. I approached close enough to look deeply into her dark eyes and I pulled out my journal and sketched her, in what felt to me a very intimate act. She didn't move, just fixed her black and yellow eyes on me.

Her markings were striking. She had a dark brown hood, a breast with brown and white crosshatching, a square patch of yellow on her cere, and a black beak below meant for serious business. Her talons were yellow like those of the hawks in our neighborhood. She was a strikingly large bird. I've always thought that because they are "falcons" peregrines were small. But that wasn't the case. She wasn't as large as a nearby caged red-tailed hawk, but she was more impressive in some way, maybe because she seemed exotic, as if a prince had just walked into a room full of peasants.

Once I finished the quick crude sketch I tried taking one step closer but the moment I approached the peregrine took off and dropped down two perches and settled near the back of the cage with her back to me.

After watching the peregrine I walked over to the red-shouldered hawk cage. I stood in front of her cage a long time. This female had been hit by a car and her wing was permanently stiffened at its side. The bird had trouble gaining the highest perches, the high limbs being one hop too far. I tried the whistle I'd perfected back home to draw her attention, to commune with the bird. I wanted her to acknowledge me. I wanted from her a gesture of connection more than I wanted it with the peregrine in front of its cage. After all, this was one of "my" birds, part of the tribe of red-shouldered hawks that tend the waterways of the East. She rested silently. She called to no one. She sat uninterested, making no movement toward responding, practicing a hawk version of the thousand-mile stare.

The injured red-shouldered hawk looked at the sky through the fencing, as if she wanted to launch, but then thought better of it and settled for a jump to another lower perch. While I watched she looked straight up five or six times. Will that ever go away? Will she always remember the sky?

30 August. My mother kept a bird in a cage for years, a cockatiel named Pretty Prince. The bird lived, as many pet birds do, a long time. It offered her companionship and emotional support. When Pretty Prince finally died, we joked that the bird had suffered from secondhand smoke. I thought of Pretty Prince as I listened to the hawks this morning. Like a sharp ledge of memory, one series of sharp cries and then silence says, *of course I'm still here.* Yes, I worry about these birds—car collisions, poisonings, old age. These hawks are never going to be in a cage. There are so many things conspiring against a wild bird of prey. The average life span of a wild red-shouldered hawk is about two years. Of course, that figures in all the fledglings killed in the nests by great horned owls and such. I've been watching game cam footage of eagles and owls raiding hawk and osprey nests, but I've had to stop. It only deepens my anxiety. One clip in particular haunts me, a night shot of a nest cam on two red-shouldered hawks preening casually, and in the distance the delta form of an approaching great horned owl can just barely be seen, closing in fast on the unsuspecting birds. One bird is plucked out of the nest and the owl keeps going. Truly, death from above.

4:00 p.m. I text my friend Drew, the ornithology professor teaching nearby. I often use him as a lifeline when I'm floating free in a sea of orno-anxiety. I want assurance from outside my perspective. Drew doesn't want to hear about my fear. He wants me to explore my curiosity.

"Ride on the buteo's back," Drew texts, then adds, "Let the poetry soar. Where would you be if you were a hawk? Think about being harassed by crows and blue jays. How would the landscape change over generations for these soaring bog buzzards?"

31 August. *—O hawk, are you ornithological? Avian? A small dinosaur, a paltry pterodactyl in the treetops singing the blues for your supper? Are you irritated? It's your prominent chord you hurl three times. You sound like a needle stuck in a groove, woodshedding the same ballad verse. What exactly are you hawking, hawk? The treetops grieve at dawn when you wake; the sky is forked by your six-note cry. Then you are done by ten, and then back again near dusk. Where do you spend the day? Some raptor equivalent of a diner? On some swamp limb, shouting down crows? Did some antediluvian slight piss you off? Or was it something Noah said?*

1 September. These hawks I follow don't seem very intent on gaining altitude. It's as if they want to keep me down in the tangle of branches, hunting with them. They want to deny me perspective. Audubon called the interior woodlands "the fittest haunts" of what he calls "the red-shouldered buzzard." (Audubon's use of "buzzard" is a throwback to what buteos are called in the Old World.) The world of these hawks seems capped at tree level. They move like the speeder bikes in *Return of the Jedi*, chasing through the forest. Drew says that because of this hunting and travel mode they suffer frequent collisions and blunt-force injuries in their line of work—broken bones and concussions are common, and they have no medical teams or concussion protocol to get them back in the game. "Their game is eat or die, and death as often as not comes from a collision."

Even their cousins, the red-tailed hawks, seem to like the wide open sky more than red-shouldered hawks. For the red-shouldered hawks there are wakes and there are tiltings, but the wakes are formed and fill much quicker. When death comes by way of a red-shouldered hawk, it comes from above, but from a tighter, shorter trajectory.

2 September. Early morning the red-shouldered hawks cry to the northeast. One series of sharp cries and then silence, as if to say, *of course I am still here.*

3 September. Moist tropical air. South of us a hurricane moves along the Georgia coast, pushing outer bands of intermittent rain our way. I keep wondering as I hear the hawk's call, What's the next step for me? How do I draw even closer to these birds? How do I observe with more than my ears? I am well into the third month of this yearlong wildlife experiment and so far I have only a few key sightings. Where is the center of the hawk's territory? Where did they last nest? How far afield do they wander? Once the days cool and the undergrowth dies back, I plan to survey the nearby woods looking for a nest. It must be out there somewhere.

6 September. This weekend at a book festival in Atlanta a friend told me a hawk story. She said she was walking in the early morning around the neighborhood when something hit her in the back of the head. She said it was still too dark to see clearly so she never saw what hit her. Next morning it happened again. This time she saw it: "A hawk dive-bombing from a tree." It hit harder the second time, and even drew blood. Undeterred, the next morning she donned her son's old football helmet and carried a stick. The dive-bomber descended again.

I asked a few questions. We determined it was a red-shouldered—stripped tail, right size. "I found out it's terrorizing the neighborhood," she said. "One man had two hats stolen off the top of his head."

8 September. It is barely dawn. Milky light through the dark trees. A pattern of light and shade that will change as the weather cools. Four cries earlier but now it's gone silent again. When we drove home last night there was a large dead copperhead on our road—probably thermoregulating on the warm pavement, then run over by a car—maybe two and a half feet long. I slumped it over a stick and moved it from the roadway. I wonder if the hawk would eat it? Now it will cool and rot in the weeds. I nearly cried. I am always filled with such sorrow for a snake.

9 September. We must bring mystery into awareness. One of the only ways to be aware is to enact sharp attention over and over, to practice.

10 September. *—I just heard your crying outside. I note your cry and sometimes follow it. I layer it with the other bird sounds and sometimes pull it like a string, stitching the morning tight for a few moments. What are you communicating? What space do you define?*

11 September. Barely light. Greasy blue sheet of late summer sky behind black trunks and leaves.

12 September. The two hawks converge like shot arrows above the flood plain. Their kee-you, kee-you, kee-you is intense and separated, but magnetic. They start below like two cranked machines and quickly follow a hidden vector to proximity. When they converge in the distance (how quickly they fly from near to far) they call back and forth with more urgency than I have heard in months. I have been listening intently ten minutes and they are far away. How would I fare in such an existence of mobile fury?

Almost noon. I hear the hawks again, as if they are checking in with each other, calling from two directions in the floodplain. It's like they are texting back and forth, "Here I am! Here I am! Here I am!" I know that the size of the home range is three and a half square kilometers. I picture what that looks like on a map, ridgetop to ridgetop.

13 September. The weather is cool in the morning now, but still stifling hot during the days. In a little over two weeks it will be October, soon too cold to sit on the deck in shorts. How will the sounds change? Will it feel so much like I am suspended within a sound cloud? The crows are stirred up. They pull the net tight with their calls. They are the characters with the most lines in this play.

15 September. This morning the truce between the hawks and the crows has ended. Somewhere in the lowland forest to the west many crows are raising hell. The noise goes on for five minutes, like a wildfire of cawing fed by gas. Then, just as fast, it's gone. Was it one of the hawks they were upset with? They can get stirred up. Now I hear the red-shouldered passing back and forth kee-youing. Not anxious at all. Maybe the dispute is settled, and the hawk is somewhere else, letting the crows bicker.

4:00 p.m. Driving home from campus I stop at a busy intersection surrounded by fast food two miles west of our house. I spot a red-shouldered hawk flying low over traffic, its flight like a clothesline strung between two poles. I pull over. It lands on top of a power pole and I watch the hawk dismantle a chipmunk above speeding cars.

17 September. Driving northwest on the upper road with my window open I hear one of the red-shouldered hawks farther away from the river than ever before. Just a few brief sharp calls and then gone. I never see the bird. I hear it move through the suburban forest. It's the sound of a can being opened, edgy as a basalt blade. If a sound could have an odor, these cries would be something softer than metal, like the ragged cracked musky husks of the hickories they fly through.

I wonder again about territories overlapping and strung end to end along the creek. I'm trying to figure it out. Are they constant? How do they work out the lines between one and another? In this study so far, there are more questions than answers, more conjecture than hard data. The rich bottomland around our house is real and it's also data rich— soundings, sightings.

19 September. Amid the early morning two-front crying of the red-shouldered hawks along the creek a barred owl tumbles silently from a poplar at the edge of the yard with a small gray squirrel in its talons. This careless, gregarious young gray squirrel should have stayed longer in its nest today. It paid with its life for rising early. Then even more silently the owl squares up, helicopters to a lower limb, and lands with its back to my curiosity. It steadies, takes a first tugging bite, then a second, and hunches slightly. Between bites the owl turns its flat face my way, like tilting a giant ear to the world. Maybe what it hears are the epochs flowing past, the vast eddies and cutbacks falling away from this moment back sixty million years. Or maybe it hears rodents in the rotting duff, a small cacophony below.

The leaves around the owl erupt in titmouse tweeting, like a dozen fire alarms. The owl seems unfazed. One adult gray squirrel shimmies down the same tree. Then, like a blade sliding back into its sheath, the owl sails toward the creek, deeper into the woods.

22 September. 7:17 a.m. Summer ends in three hours. Yellow is already the dominant color in the poplars. Leaves fall with regularity. The gray squirrels gather heaps for nesting. Surely autumn is some solace for hunting birds, as their dark eyes will see farther once the leaves fall. Their green tangled world will be augmented with open spaces. I hear a blue jay in the front yard, a rare visitor here, for it prefers the open wooded lots of the larger subdivision to the north, and a pileated woodpecker calls. No one with good sense enters autumn alone.

Fall

23 September. I have decided my hawking tactics must change. I can't sit on the porch and simply listen for the cries of these birds near and far. I must follow the birds out into their world.

Maybe I'll try biking, like Baker. It's been a week. After this long string of silent days, I couldn't wait for the hawks to come to me, so I resorted to literary conjuring. It's before ten in the morning, and still cool enough to enjoy a bike ride. I pull my old bike out of the garage, pump up the knobby tires, sling my binoculars over my back, and set off through the neighborhood.

I set out to carve a figure eight formed of listening. Though it's good exercise, I'm hoping my excursion will activate a hawk show too, and, of course, in the back of my mind, I still haven't given up on finding the nest, if there is one. I roll first northeast, climbing a little, then turn in the cul-de-sac and head back southwest, reversing my path. I put my head down and listen to birdsong, piling up the melodies of cardinal and titmice as I blast by.

A lot has changed since Baker tracked his hawks from the seat of a bike. Mine is a mountain model made for the trails—with front and back shocks, a little overkill now on these suburban streets. Baker's bike, I imagine, was the common British issue commuter with road tires, no frills, like you'd see in postwar countryside villages when cars and petrol were still luxuries, black maybe, with handlebars like longhorns. My handlebars are straight across and made for stooping on hill climbs and downhill glides.

Where do the birds sit? The sky has no property lines, but the neighborhood does, from the postage-stamp subdivision lots to the large private tract along the creek. My large-tract neighbors have posted signs to prohibit trespassing. They have little interest in the hawks. If I follow the hawks there I must do it by stealth.

24 September. Last night about ten p.m. we found ourselves enmeshed in a chorus of evening clowns—at least three barred owls hooting in the night, a ruckus, steady loud laughing, hooting, and gargling, alternating, accelerating challenges triangulating from dark tree line to tree line.

Year-round residents like the red-shouldereds, the barred owls mate for life. (Or so we think.) The owls have been a presence in our woods since we moved in years ago, but last night was an unusually spirited chorus, so loud and constant, bouncing through the trees in our front yard, that it drew us outside to marvel and listen.

We stood and looked up. The dark shadow of a moving bird passed in front of the streetlight. Soon the line of vocal engagement shifted too, with the advancing owl flinging new choruses into the dark and the answering owl moving back a tree or two. Friendly songfest, flirtation, or home-range challenge? The misty yellow neighborhood lights blinked out as leaves shifted in a slight breeze. The sky above us closed in, a shrinking horizon seen from below. The year's first autumnal night exhaled, and the owls called again.

25 September. This morning I slipped on my muck boots and walked due west into the bottoms beyond our house seeking the hawks. Our property extends out into the bottoms, but I was off our four acres quickly, a little south of where the surveyors staked our line years ago. Most of the year it's too wet to be there, recurrent inundation keeping the soils moist. Every time the creek slips over the banks the water floods in, depositing another layer of red clay.

Right now the soil is pocked with the twin crescents of heavy deer traffic, the forest floor's still soupy in places, and canopied with heavy timber—ash, sweet gum, box elder, and a large number of swamp chestnuts. The understory is mostly privet and native switch cane in patches, sometimes eight feet tall. Segmented like the familiar exotic bamboo but more flexible, our native cane is slender and delicate, swaying slightly now in the breeze. The privet offers browse for the deer in winter.

I find a grove of inviting hardwoods to surround me. I prop my Crazy Creek chair against a decaying log. The layers of leaves break the midday light into spots of shadow and silver beams. Leaves filter me from above, as if the forest is an open sea and I, a diver below.

This is mature timber, with some trees too big to get my arms around. The swamp chestnut oaks along the creek here have always fascinated me. We have several big ones at the back of our yard, but here they live hybrid lives in and out of the water. Their acorns are huge, and in the big mast years they are deer candy. The nuts are the diameter of a quarter and contain a lower dose of tannin, so are less bitter to the forest browsers.

One of the titmice has decided to announce to the outside world, or at least its tribe, that I have settled in. Actually there are surprisingly few birds here at this early hour—there is one I can't seem to get my ears around, scolding persistently from the high branches. A warbler, maybe? Probably migrating through—"whiz-lizzy-lizzy-lizzy." And a crow is somewhere too, making that familiar croak.

My intention is to get to know the bottoms better, as many mornings like this one I hear the red-shouldered hawks crying from this direction but seldom track them outward. I am hoping to see an old nest, or catch sight of a bird on a perennial perch, but nothing that dramatic happens, as the birds are nowhere to be seen or heard.

But I'm not patient enough. Farther off to the south a red-shouldered hawk calls. I hope the bird will come my way. Will I get lucky and my perch in the deep woods intersect with the fluid world of its hunting?

And then it flies toward me. It's hard to track the bird with my ears, which lack the dimension of distance. Then I hear another hawk. They seem to come from the north, converging, like one side of a vice closing on me. The hawks close in—loud, fluid—and only a hundred yards away. Will they land right above me? Will I see them up close?

26 September. Yesterday I ended abruptly with questions. The hawks never approached any closer. This morning, the hawks are once again both present and distant, faint cries only, thin wires of presence cast from the outermost edge of their home range.

It was dark an hour ago and now it's light. The crows have the early stage, and the Carolina wrens compete with construction equipment across the river. The harsh grinding of bulldozers is as real as birdsong. Some would call this an Anthropocene soundtrack, since few moments in the suburban woods are without human sounds. The red-shouldered hawks live within this modern mesh as well. They hear it. It computes. They, as well as we, are now complicit in its narrative.

29 September. Away for three days. In the distance, due south, across the creek (a new direction for them), I hear one of the red-shouldered hawks, the three-step cry like a burner sputtering on simmer. I can barely parse it against the distant ambient human evening score of motorcycles, accelerating cars, backfires, dog barks, and train clangs. Closer by, the crows, cardinals, titmice, and nuthatches spark my attention's wavering flame.

All day I had an uneasy feeling of dread and then a friend posted that his wife, long-suffering with cancer, had finally died. My grief is a flue, shadowed, like the woods below getting dark. I find no comfort in the black cinder of a chickadee's hooded head passing in and out from behind the feeder.

1 October. Noon. The cobalt blue sky to the north above the ridge is full of soaring birds right now and the resident red-shouldered hawks aren't happy about it. I hear their cries, north and south. High in the sky there are two turkey vultures, one black vulture, and what may be two broad-winged hawks carving large loops, thermal-aided, climbing high up the dome of this first October sky. One of the red-shouldered hawks leaves the closed confines of the backyard forest and soars above, crying kwee, kwee, kwee the whole time. I spot it through slanting sunlight and the fragile drying canopy of the autumn tulip poplar. A challenge to the interloper from the north? A trumpeter of settled life below? Soon the high soaring birds are so distant they vanish.

2 October. Sunday morning in the floodplain. Walking in, I scared one of the red-shouldered hawks off a low perch on a big tulip poplar; it lifted and glided in one deft motion—but then I saw one of the barred owls sitting right above where the hawk had perched in a higher crotch. The big owl turned the wide platter of its face toward me, unconcerned.

I settle again in my camp chair in the old spot from the week before in the ancient grove under the swamp chestnut. The owl moves soundlessly from tree to tree above me. These two birds—the hawk and the owl—are like two sides of a worn coin. They fill the same niche, one during the day, the other at night. The barred owl is even called the nocturnal equivalent of the red-shouldered hawk. Even though I know this is true, I didn't expect to find them resting so close to each other.

The breeze stirs and the big owl moves perpendicular to the falling leaves—yellow, black, gold, chocolate, drifting down like snow. I look upward through the binoculars and the canopy twists into focus. On the rough bark of the trunk of the big tree in which the owl had sat only moments before, cross vines cling like exposed veins. All around me are hornbeam, tulip poplar, ash, box elder, and an understory thick with privet and holly.

I sit for fifteen minutes dead still, as four deer—two does and two fawns—walk past. They stop, stomp, huff, and start through the privet. They watch this yellow-shirted interloping listener in their woods.

Is he as crazy? They huff. I have never witnessed deer quite this long. And then in the distance, to the south, the red-shouldered cries. It hasn't moved closer since I sat down.

3 October. The sky clouds up and the air transmogrifies, from summer's soppy weight to crisp and cool. The songbirds have been feeding in the three hours since dawn in the newly filled seed tubes. A nuthatch makes a foray to the feeder from the black gum tree. In the surrounding oaks and poplars squadrons of seed-sated titmice chatter like typewriters. Below, six nervous deer wander through the lower yard from east to west like rag pickers; four of them are probably the same deer I surprised in the privet yesterday morning. They pause and kick in the fallen leaves, competing with two brash gray squirrels for the cast-off seeds I scattered there, rooting around, then licking the caramel-colored mineral block below the fence before retreating into the woods along their almost invisible throughway.

My brother-in-law lives on the other side of the creek, about a half mile upstream. Yesterday we were over there briefly and when I was standing in the yard I heard the kwee, kwee, kwee of a red-shouldered hawk from the floodplain below. Was it one of "our" hawks or another competing hawk cruising the leading edge of yet another circle strung like a line of platters along every southern waterway? For a human the idea of territory is complex. The coffee I sip as I contemplate the cries of hawks in this piedmont floodplain is "fair trade" from Ethiopia, and the cream comes from the faraway Midwest.

All hawks are locavores. This morning before breakfast I rescued a tiny thin ring-neck snake floundering on the driveway, dust-covered and disoriented by the cool morning. Maybe it crawled there yesterday evening when the pavement was warm and stayed too long before retreating? A sharp-eyed hawk could have made breakfast of it.

7 October. Heavy rain today. Gray cotton clouds blot the sun. Another hurricane churns up the coast to the south, promising a storm surge in the low country and bands of heavy rain here. I fill up the feeders, and a ravenous band of titmice and chickadees are hard at it, lowering the level of oiled seeds by the hour. The yard's resident Carolina wrens also are active in spite of the steady downpour.

The last time I heard the hawks was yesterday evening, a single cry from the south, one note, followed by a plaintive kee-yer, kee-yer, kee-yer. Where do they shelter on such dreary days? Do they perch and wait it out? Is the hunting ever decent on such a wet day?

8 October. The air smells like wet straw. The sky glows like a lamplit burlap sack. Branches lash back and forth with each pulse of wind. The hurricane passes along the coast. I check the online weather station and the barometric pressure is the lowest I've seen it here—28.81 inches. How do birds respond to this falling pressure? "Shelter in place" is the advice circulating online to the members of my species with coastal homes.

Birds are sensitive to weather. Migrating white-throated sparrows adjust their behavior when the pressure drops, but what of resident hawks that don't leave? Some scientists have theorized that all birds have an avian barometer that senses pressure changes. They also might be alerted to approaching storms by "infrasound"—low-frequency noise—produced by an approaching storm. What must a storm sound like to a resident hawk? It must be enough to shake up the daily routines. Somewhere in the floodplain the hawks are hunkered with wings pulled tight. When a storm hits, a songbird can simply land on a branch or a wire, and their talons close upon contact and remain closed by default until the bird chooses to fly away. Is the same true of a hawk? I hope as the weather clears today the foraging birds return.

9 October. 6:00 a.m. The hawk cries draw me out into the wet woods, and I follow. I walk from the backyard into the floodplain with my notebook, as I have done on three Sunday mornings in a row now. I sit on the ground again, back in my private grove, my poet's tree stand, surrounded by the big swamp chestnut, the green ash, the sweet gums, sheltered down low by an ironwood twisted and old, its tough gray veined bark splotched with patches of blue.

Today there is more birdsong—maybe because the storm has passed and the birds are moving, hungry, impatient, and weather irritated, but it's not irritation I hear in their calls. It is perseverance, steadiness, business-going-on-through-the-eons-as-usual presence.

Three blue jays check me out too. One calls three times right over my head. Blue jays are not something I see regularly at our house, but maybe I am sitting on the edge of their home range now—the lawns to the west where there are abundant water oaks full of acorns. Or maybe they are migrating too, and had to hunker down and wait out the storm, and now are feeding before heading south?

This month the woods are an ocean, and I surf them. Birdsong is a tide approaching from the north, a storm surge as the passerines migrate through, bound for South America. They pass over me like raindrops. They fly through the branches like wind. They perch and chatter around me. But I can't forget the bird feeder regulars—the titmice. They scold me from nearby box elders, wondering, I am sure, why I have left the refuge of my screened porch to cower here in the privet.

11 October. Cold on the backside of the hurricane (forty-four degrees) and no breeze, as if the distant storm has sucked all movement through summer's final straw. I heard the red-shouldered early this morning west of here in the floodplain—one cry, a bookmark slipped between the two colliding seasons.

12 October. I drove out of the subdivision before dawn and a coyote crossed in front of my truck. The song-dog was impatient to be somewhere. I wanted to follow. I turned left along the ridge, but it soon disappeared between the dark houses, reappearing moments later, a specter, phantom, wraith, spirit. The coyote's coat was mottled gray and black. It could have been my headlights but the end of its tail seemed dipped in silver. All this while the hawks slept.

13 October. Agitated and communal, the crows hover on the edge of the day, a coal cloud barbed with threats, their voices like needles piercing the trees' foliating leaves. Then silence. Where did the crows go? How did this snarl of caws collapse into only the ambient rattle of a bulldozer in the distance?

19 October. A red-shouldered hawk sat on a power pole a half mile downstream from the house. One of my birds? And then ten minutes later, another red-shouldered hawk soared in slow looping glides above the retention pond on the ridge-top. The outer edge of their living circle? The hawk's shadow tightened on the grass as I pulled off to take notes.

Then, at home for lunch, I heard the red-shouldered hawks in the bottoms to the southwest. Were those other hawks with nearby territories? And then, across the sky cut a hawk, a bent bow, a ranging horn, a set of scissors trimming the fat of midday.

20 October. The hawks are a rasping wake-up call. The swamp woods west of the house seem to be the hawks' autumn roost retreat. A hawk must gather the shortening day. A hawk must see to live. Light is first, and nothing stalls the hawk's seasonal hunger. Before dawn deer rustle in the dark under the swamp chestnut oak, cracking acorns the size of thumbs. The deer are fat this October, browsing the near woods.

23 October. Coldest morning of the year, thirty-eight degrees, and the hawks and crows are at war again. A large oak west of the house roils with black avengers coming and going. If crows had battleships, they'd call them in. The morning lights up with the crow missiles. But the hawks hold out, perched in the same tree. They sword duel. They crack back with rifle-butt vocals. They hurl hand-grenade defenses. They scream bloody murder, and the crows give it back. I watch from the side yard. The sickle-shaped crows drift in and out against the blue morning sky.

24 October. I'm reading a book called *Poetic Animals and Souls* by Randy Malamud. It's about the relationship between people and animals and how it's always been hierarchical and impermeable in novels and poems. "We are here and they are there."

In the Great Chain of Being, Malamud claims, other animals have always been considered inferior to human beings. Civilization is privileged. The lives of animals are commodified, or exterminated altogether. They are a means to an end. Animals "stake out the perimeter" of the culture. "If we are interested in animals, we are inclined to bring them into our world rather than meeting them on their own terms, and in their own territory."

But what if in the case of the red-shouldered hawks our territories are one and the same? Can their terms be my terms? Can the borderline be nonexistent? Where are the borders for the suburban hawks?

This hawk journal creates the sense, at least for a year, of the hawks always being here, flying outward over and through many circles of my awareness daily. No containment. No constraint. How could a human constrain a wild hawk within its own home range anyway?

26 October. I don't know why exactly, but this morning the world feels wounded. There is sadness in the trees. Each time the hawks cry, they spread it. They sound like whiners. Am I overinterpreting their vocals? The crows are conspirators or competitors or something I can't explain with my mammal vocabulary.

29 October. It's my birthday. Sixty-two years old. I have outlived J. A. Baker.

30 October. Sunday morning. I am back sitting in the floodplain grove again. Yesterday I was on a hike with a friend at a lake and a red-shouldered hawk landed on the nearby crosspiece of an array of purple martin gourds. "I've found these hawks to be curious of me," he said, and I was jealous. He told several stories of his intimate interactions over time. He said he'd seen them eating crayfish along the edge of the lake. The bird we watched rotated its head and checked us out then dropped from the crosspiece on a small creature below and disappeared into the brush along the lake edge.

Tomorrow is Halloween. Isn't that when all things take flight? Maybe the ghosts of raptors past will fill the evening skies.

Sightings and imaginings pile up. Curious shadowy conjectures flock in my mind. I hear a mower start up, and I go avian and avoid the nearby neighbors out doing chores; I go flying, and move quietly above their homes. I am as inconspicuous as the hawks I seek. I am imperceptible, folded into the suburban day so fully that when I pass over I might as well be the wind. I rise into the living body of a hawk, then I land in a tree to perch patiently, to sight along the narrowed barrel of my native vision until some prey moves and I lock down and drift from above and seize it—snake, lizard, mouse, mole, or shrew. Among the river cane and privet hedges I settle in, my life in full flight.

31 October. 7:30 a.m. A Halloween hawk calls. Screeching low.

1 November. Before dawn a barred owl's single scream competes with the steady rhythm of crickets. It's warm and I sit on the side porch in shirtsleeves. This fall is so unusual with the drought and unseasonable temperatures. I remember that counting the number of cricket chirps in fourteen seconds and adding forty gives you the air temperature. What's that? Sixty-four? Right on, the weather app confirms. There are predictable rhythms in nature—heartbeats, breathing, the rise and fall of the sun—but how many times can you count one thing and accurately predict another? Knowing natural history is a fine thing, but paying attention is the key. Noticing until it becomes mundane and then noting what is novel. Love is attention, and love is noting what you love and how you love it.

I love my wife, our house, our family, and our marriage. It has spanned almost twenty years now. Such commitment wasn't always easy for me. I was married briefly one other time, in my twenties, and it didn't go so well. My first wife was a competitive runner, and I ran with her. This morning I thought of a short story I once wrote in which I imagined climbing inside her runner's heart and riding there, to somehow see if she loved me. "Then I would know whether I should leave," I wrote. "I would smell it in her blood, salty and thin, as it circulated through her body on the run. I would hang there in her heart by my hands, like doing a pull-up, and wait for the message from her returning blood. Or I would ride there inside her in a small boat like a kayak. It's called a bloodstream, surely, I thought, it must go someplace, to some safe harbor where we could sit and talk honestly, safely for the first time in months. Was she willing to let me in? Was her heart open? Had it grown large enough with all her running?"

Maybe it's a silly fantasy to ride around in another's heart, but it points to how important fantasy can be, how it can point you in the right direction, how dreaming can become the portal we can walk through into real life, not fantasy. My life with Betsy has been made real through our long commitment. We walk the same trails over and over. We have slowed down to a livable pace. But none of that is boring. Our love is still exciting, and this place offers opportunities every day to deepen my understanding of relationships. When I chase the hawks I am chasing my dreams.

2 November. Lunchtime. An early fog has lifted, leaving a vault of milky blue skies. Alternating raptors fill out the afternoon. A red-tailed hawk skirts the river crying leisurely, a long chirrrrrrr, and just downstream the sky is peppered with silent turkey vultures soaring in looping rope swings. The forest around me has turned banana yellow overnight. The sourwoods have turned mango, and the scarlet oaks drip strawberry and plum. Finally fall has punched its ticket. The ground where I step is brittle with drifts of fallen leaves. In a week the sky will fill the horizon again wherever I look.

6:00 p.m. —*Finally you show up. Where the hell you been? I've endured the soaring vultures and carpetbagging red-tails all day but here you finally are at suppertime, singing your heart out. I missed your pluck and the territory you travel on a single tune. Swamp eagle, sky-screamer, bog-buzzard, bellboy to the heavens, I listen to you like a retreating train headed away. Maybe your belly is full of snake paying the price for some unlucky sunning on a parched November day. Did you hear the red-tail earlier and want to challenge it like a character from* West Side Story? *It's not a show tune you sing. Not enough narrative line there for that. Your cry is more like a fire alarm.*

5 November. Dull shadows soften the coal black branches of the hardwoods. The early cry of a red-shouldered hawk north of the house has shifted this cold morning (forty-five degrees). When I hear it, I grab my binoculars and follow my love, rush up the driveway. There is something subdued about this cry, something plaintive, a new register of notes for these gregarious loud-mouthed birds. Then as I walk another red-shouldered hawk sweeps above, moving from south to north. That black silhouette carves past like a scythe and disappears in the trees ahead. While I am looking up, clutches of small birds flee, heading south to north. The early morning light floods the gaps between branches where the leaves used to clot them with green.

6 November. Sunday morning. A turkey vulture soars in the distance, like a black thread pulled by a needle through the disrobing hardwoods. As if on cue, a red-shouldered hawk breaks into cry up the creek, and a gray squirrel chants disapproval from a nearby swamp chestnut oak. Then the squirrel chorus starts up in earnest—point-counterpoint all over the floodplain in a widening circle around me. I hear that sound they make when relaxing, a creaking gate, a rusty-hinged croak with a lift at the end. I am back in my camp chair, in my Sunday meditation spot. Occasionally songbirds move through—is it the back edge of the fall migration or just-arrived winter residents? Their songs add some punctuation to the conversation. Chipping notes tossed in like periods, commas, colons, and dashes. Drew, my ornithologist friend, would know them all by their songs.

Drought continues. Another week without rain. Last fall I would have been sitting in four inches of standing water. The clouds drift west to east: fleecy, dry feathers, more frill than function.

If I sit here long enough maybe the songbirds will grow curious and gather around as if I'm Saint Francis. Several small birds stay just out of sight but I hear their wings fluttering in the privet. Sometimes when the leaves flutter I hope it's whole flights of birds settling in. I long to merge with the mysterious winged world, be it buzzard, songbird, or hawk. Who is eating seeds from the sweet gum balls high up? Show yourself more clearly, you small foragers in dull gold overcoats. Come down so I can lay binoculars on you. What complaint does that distant crow have? Come share it. Come divide your forage with me, your distant bipedal cousin with his back to a rotting log.

Enough pleading. I might pack it in. The edge of morning now bleeds into midday. Daylight savings time. Tinkering with Creation for convenience. Time's arrow slowed. Time to circle back. I am hungry already. Is my hunger real? More real than this?

7 November. *—I wish I had bat ears. Then every day I would know where you are. This morning it was thirty-seven degrees at seven a.m. I think I heard you off to the northeast, but it could have been a blue jay, as they like to mimic. I am sitting in the cold on the deck (now nine a.m.) but I don't care. You are probably sitting somewhere too, warming up, or are you on the wing, taking a lap? Is it possible to make a story if the hero never shows? Is it probable to shape a narrative out of absence or, at best, the protagonist sighted through autumn branches on a flight from here to there? I'm not happy with this cast of sighing gray squirrels or the*

chickadees bent on emptying the tube feeder. I want you to be
John Wayne, to take over, and shift this slow tale toward the
middle acts. I need trouble, the only thing that pulls a reader
along. Where's the jeopardy to hawk watching?

3:00 p.m. A flock of wild turkeys walks through the yard
at three p.m. There must be twenty. They are thorough in
their woodland exploration. No leaf is left unturned. The turkeys cruise through, low and in first gear, not in a hurry at all.
They're on a stroll. Then a hawk flies over. It's close enough
I see the checkerboard of brown and white on its flanks. I
swear it glances askance at me, cocks its head, and we see eye
to eye. The big FP alarm (feathered predator) shoots through
all the gray squirrels below. They scatter and set up a pattern
of pitiful squeaks that echo from tree to tree. But as quick
and as quietly as it comes, the hawk is gone.

8 November. Election morning. I have returned from
voting. I was the first in line. I can assume the hawks don't
care whom I voted for, but I believe the planet should, and
so the hawks should too. But listening for the hawks puts so
much in perspective. The hawks let loose. Keer, keer, keer,
back and forth through the bottoms like an alarm.

10 November. Early and chilly. Heard both hawks west
of the house. One seemed disturbed, the cries manic. I have
been depressed for two days, not listening to the world.
The hawks are even more subdued. I wish I had time to
investigate. They seem more present this morning. I'm
looking forward to the Christmas holidays, when I can take
off after them. If I sought them more would they be more
forthcoming?

The pawpaws along the floodplain edge are patterned
yellow and green, tropical ears lolling in the breeze. It's only
with plants that I have developed rapport.

14 November. I go outside when I hear crows, but no
hawks for three days now. The skies are filled with smoke
from wildfires to the west. Thousands of acres of mountain
land are burning. My eyes hurt, and I am sneezing. The
drought has lasted forty-five days in some counties up there.

Some say the fires are arson, though it doesn't matter. The forests burn no matter what started them. I don't remember such fires in my lifetime. Satellite photos show the plume of smoke swirling over us like a mare's tail. We had our first bit of relief here yesterday, less than half an inch of rain, but the mountain front kept the moisture pinched in the piedmont.

But it was a good day in spite of the smoke. Earlier, driving home from school, I watched a small murmuration of grackles wheeling over an empty field, then noticed some crows stirred up about something on the ground. A northern harrier, what I have always called a marsh hawk, coursed low in front of me—white rump patch, buoyant, with wings raised in a V—rowing along the motorway until it landed in a tree.

16 November. If I were a researching ornithologist I would now have another bankable data point on my home-range map in the southeast quadrant, the most empty of the hawk territories, a little-known suburb of my attention. It's been five days since I last heard one of the hawks and I've missed them—a long absence from what I know of them so far. And then another hawk calls from the east! Then, after this tease, they glide further away. What perch calls them to it?

17 November. A hawk is back on the west side of the house this morning—noisy, persistent, gregarious. A hundred miles to our west the fires still burn. Sometimes with the election and the smoke I feel the whole world is on fire.

21 November. 9:10 a.m. The coldest morning of the year so far. I take out the garbage. I do the simplest of human chores. And then I see both of the red-shouldered hawks just northeast of the house, one perched on the neighbor's tree, the other perched on a big oak in the vacant lot. They exchange calls for a few minutes and then pass over and I see them up close. It's like one of those moments when the fighter flies low enough to see the pilot in the cockpit. The hawks are bright like the morning, bright in the sun, and I can even see the banding on the tails. I listen to them calling in the margins of the yard.

28 November. —*I have heard you crying each to each (like just now) on these cold mornings but I have lately stayed inside. A week without your songs, notes flung not at me but only against the forest and the sky. The leaves have fallen, almost revealing the river through the trees, our seasonal vista. My attention is a rookery only to my own fears and needs. Today I contain no territory, save what is already settled. There are no fields of flight big enough for birds. There are no stationary perches low in the canopy for me to land on. There are only views shortened by foliage, but they are smoky and colored not by autumn but by my own deficits, not yours. What will it take to enter the woods as an old man? To molt? What draws the arrow out after it enters curiosity's flesh? Crow caws. A solitary note, answered by a hawk. Is this some new sound, or more of the same?*

4:00 p.m. Scary moment—a hawk just flew into our big side window. It pulled up soon enough to avoid a hard, maybe deadly collision, but was it injured? I walked outside and scanned the grounds. No slumped carcass. No hobbled, broken bird the color of fallen leaves. It seems to have survived.

30 November. After heavy rains yesterday I rode around in the truck looking deep into the thinning fall woods with the curtain of leaves slumped to the forest floor on all sides, opening up a hidden fringe of trees and limbs. I searched for the silhouettes of perched hawks waiting out the lingering wind. I hoped to catch a glimpse of one of the hawks to allay my fear that the bird who flew into my window was injured. Was the bird sitting somewhere concussed like a linebacker going through protocol? I saw nothing but wet crotches of oak and hickory. That chorus of crows out of tune—is it an owl or the hawks they seek to pester into flight? Three, four, five crows glided overhead, their brethren chortling in the distance. Then nine more: black bodies headed in the opposite direction. Were these resident corvids or an uninvited platoon from outside, a D-Day landing in the trees? Then the first turkey vulture drifted over too, riding the wind, its fingered black wings like crows, only larger. These were good breezes they marshaled. They played above. I worried below. What if the hawks go away and I lose track of them? Are the crows enough? Would my data mining survive the catastrophe of a dead bird? With hawks living among houses there will always be that fear.

1 December. Sky the color of faded blue jeans. Fog in the bottoms. The tumult of last night's storm leaves the ground soaked again, the second rainstorm in three days after fifty-one official days of drought. I step onto the back deck to eat my cereal and one of the red-shouldered hawks lifts off from a branch right over the garden pond and glides to a tree limb a little further away. I'm relieved. My fear diminishes when I hear the second hawk calling a few hundred yards away.

2 December. There is an interloper. A red-tailed hawk sits in a nearby oak in the yard stirring things up. The air smells wet and chilled from the soaking of two days' rain. The gravel lights up in the paths. Crows arrive. For a few minutes I stand and watch as the crows turn the treetops into their own battlefront. This is no corvid caucus, more Celtic war council. I watch the murder of crows dive-bombing the hawk from overhead. The hawk looks up annoyed but doesn't flinch. If this is a war, it's one as ancient as the birds themselves.

Such harassment is common if you're a lounging hawk. The field guides call it "mobbing," and there is something irrational about it. What sparks it? Sometimes the crows and hawks coexist in the same patch of woods. Other times riots of harassment break out at a hawk's mere presence on a wire or limb. Of course, the simple answer is that the activity is "antipredatory aggression" meant to save young crows from hungry hawks.

Soon the hawk has had enough. With strong intermittent beats and glides it disappears south toward the floodplain. The mob disperses. The crows call it quits and head off to other appointments. They recede over the treetops, flecks of black pepper against the milky blue morning sky.

5 December. I am caught in a diving bell of birdsong—a large flock of robins moving through. They flush among the trees like a bold flood. They twitter and surge, following the creek. I focus on one sycamore snag in which they settle. At one limb juncture there is a hollow where rainwater has gathered and they take turns bathing there, lining up like boys at a water fountain. One robin's breast is so red I doubt my identification for a moment. Maybe I have mistaken for common robins a flock of tropical birds drawn north by last week's high winds. I watch them for a while and hear a hawk again. So I walk down next to the creek, a place I know I shouldn't be, as the hunters often move back and forth on the road this season. I am alone with the robins and the blue sky and the creek is a little high. And then I hear the hawk again, calling in the distance to the west. Then I hear a second one due north of the house. Closer. More distinct, calling five, six, seven times. Those twin cries. Calling and then settling silently. I see one hawk needling through the distant trees to the west. The hawk's flight stitches together the far trees.

The closer hawk calls again and I move toward it until I spot it resting in the sun high in an oak. It's the size and shape of a football settled on the limb. The hawk calls and the more distant hawk answers. Call-and-response. And then everything goes quiet. Through my binoculars the bird looks pink and brown as the light hits it. It twists its bony head and looks down at me. It looks away and then looks at me again. I sit down to watch. I am determined to stay with this bird as long as I can. I watch it preening. Small birds move in and out of the branches: titmice, chickadees. The hawk sits untroubled. I sit for fifteen minutes and watch. The ground is wet and soaks through my pants. I lie back on the leaves. The hawk sits silently, then lets go twelve paired cries. Kee-yer, kee-yer, kee-yer. Then eighteen more. When there is no answer the hawk glides north on strong wings, out of my field of vision. I stand up and go inside.

6 December. As I follow the hawks I run into a neighbor walking his dog. He is curious about why I am out with binoculars, looking up into the trees in the middle of the day. "Oh, those hawks," he says. "They hang out at our house all the time. They sit on the gutters and look down into our front yard."

His house is northeast of ours, with a large fenced backyard. He says he once saw a hawk chasing something through their open back porch, and another time he watched one sitting on his fence a long time. "It's like it was hunting back there but I have never saw it catch anything." I tell him the hawks, if they are red-shouldereds, are probably looking for reptiles and amphibians from their perch, as his front yard has a nice moist swale planted with horsetail. "They also like to sit on the bird feeder in the backyard," he says. "Behind your house they're probably looking for birds," I answer. "They eat a few." He seems surprised by these red-shouldereds' varied culinary habits. "One time one sat for an hour on the feeder as gray squirrels ran all over below. I wondered about that."

Back behind their house is where the high ground begins, and I imagine that beyond those woods the red-tailed hawks hold sway on the higher ridge. "I am keeping a record of every time I hear them," I tell him.

"Well, have at it," he says sounding a little skeptical.

7 December. At sunrise, I'm sitting on our deck. Above, a last few bright stars. A lingering tropical air mass makes it warm enough to be in shirtsleeves, but on Friday night it's supposed to plunge into the twenties. Weather offers a reliable narrative on the certainty of change.

8 December. Today, I'm thinking about paleontology. There isn't much of a fossil record for birds. Ancient bird history is hard to reconstruct from the few fossil bones, and because of their ability to move between watersheds by flight, it's even hard to pin down the ancient origins of bird species. There are no fixed regions, no certain territories where birds have always lived. When ornithologists like Drew think of bird populations, they think in terms of "fluid faunas." I love the term—the idea that there are no geographical boundaries for birds. Instead the boundaries flow, warp, and weave, like moving cold fronts. As a species these red-shouldered hawks are limited by their diets, not some fixed line or boundary. They are creatures of the bottoms, or of the margins bounded by bottoms, what are known as "mesic" environments.

We know a little about red-shouldered hawks in the southeast through fossils, though—fossil bones have been found in a sinkhole in the Bahamas and in a Pleistocene and early Holocene tar seep in Cuba, evidence that in colder, dryer times they ranged further south, though neither the Bahamas nor Cuba has any resident red-shouldered hawks today. The species' disappearance from Cuba is a mystery. There seemed to be plenty of suitable bottomland forests to sustain these riparian-loving hawks. Maybe their disappearance was prey related, but no one knows for sure. Red-tailed hawks and broad-winged hawks are common in Cuba, but the only red-shouldered hawks there are found in fossil deposits.

9 December. More and more I find myself, like a hawk, just listening and watching. Midday on a chilly Friday, home from school for lunch, I was sitting on the screened porch, my midcanopy perch, and a leaf blower wailing in the distance. The crows called back and forth to the southwest, competing with the machinery for my attention. I hoped if I sat there long enough the hawks would check in too. When the blower ceased, it was quiet enough that I could at least distinguish signal from noise.

Driving in to work in the morning I slowed down and looked deep into the forest, inventorying trees in the floodplain, scouting the right credentials for a nest site. Lately I have been thinking again about the coming nesting season. When will the courting behavior begin? When will they nest? I'm guessing March or April will be a busy time. These days do they just perch somewhere and soak up the midday heat? I imagine their prey base shifts to small mammals as the cold moves in.

9 December. What a difference it makes for hawk watching when the leaves fall. This morning I walked out into the driveway and I heard one of the red-shouldered hawks crying to the northeast, and I focused in the direction of the call and soon saw the bird perched high in a sweet gum in my neighbor's front yard. Twenty minutes later, when I pulled out of the driveway, the hawk was still there. Only as the truck approached did it finally glide into the woods behind my neighbor's house. Now the crows are back, sounding a corvid alarm. The hawk must still be nearby, though it could be a number of unseen disturbances "here below" that set them off.

10 December. —*The sky's blue has deepened overnight. Now it has the cast of a tropic ocean. A cold wind blows and stray leaves filter to the forest floor outside the windows. I've been wondering what it's like inside your heads as the days shorten and the fields cool off. Can you feel drifting thermoclines as you coast from suburban yard to road to thinning woods? In full summer do the leaves exhale a moist breath of the forest as you drift overhead? And what of me going about my life? Who is this human whistling at you every day as if he's impersonating a hawk? Do the roads look like cursive writing from your perch? Are the trees a Japanese sumi painting as the light shifts?*

11 December. First light saw scattered waves of small dark birds moving downstream between the yard and the river. They were like a shower of scraps borne by a breeze. The cold light filtered through the branches. At dawn hunters upstream at the duck pond threw a salvo of shot at the descending flocks, casting a pall over the forest, at least for this nonhunter. The cardinals, titmice, and nuthatches feast at the feeders, unfazed. A single red-headed woodpecker inches down a trunk in the yard. Where do the hawks roost in the cold?

13 December. The span of a bird's life across the single arc of a year, that's what I want this journal to be. I want to get to the end of the year and to have captured these hawks

traveling in the amber of my prose. I will try to record everything true about them—what they eat, what they sound like,
where they roost, where they hunt.

As of this morning I've been at it a few days over five
months—not quite halfway there yet, but enough to claim a
commitment.

14 December. I've just watched *Kestrel's Eye*, a striking
documentary by the Swedish filmmaker Mikael Kristersson
made in 1999. It's about a very stark, beautiful place along
the Scandinavian seacoast where a pair of kestrels live in a
church steeple. It's a normal human place, active, cared for.
Two birds roost in the steeple and nest in a cavity. They raise
a brood of five chicks in one of the holes in the stone face.
That's all the documentary is—hunting, perching, watching,
waiting, raising chicks, for a full year, starting with winter.

The most powerful part of the film is the juxtaposition of
bird life with human life. The birds live their lives "above,"
utilizing a church, a sacred human space. They patrol a sec-
ular human space. Over the course of the year, joggers, children, cars, and a parade pass below. The birds stare down
at the church cemetery, where the living routinely tend the
graves of the dead.

The film is quiet. The soundtrack is simply the ambient
noise—falcon, chicks, the muffled voices of the humans
in their world alone, mechanical sounds of car horns and
alarms, the regular striking of the church bells. But the
sound is appropriate. There are other species—starlings,
sparrows, an endless supply of voles, and one lizard the
birds bring back from their hunting forays in the nearby
fields.

There's a real sense in this film of "Oh, this is how it all
goes." There is an obvious pared-down sense of life as the
birds live it—it's all watching, hunting, sex, raising the
young, and more watching. Everything is minimal, as it must
have felt for our species at one point in our evolutionary
path. Shelter, food, cultural interaction, and responsibilities
have now grown into a huge superstructure. That's really

clear when watching something as tiny as the tending of the geometric landscape of the graves laid out below.

At the film's conclusion the five surviving chicks begin to fledge. They've left the brood cavity and are now perched in a recessed circle above a wedding party. One of the hawk parents brings the adolescent birds a vole, which one nibbles and then drops on the party below, and another lifts a leg and shits. Kristersson stays true to his point of view and doesn't show displeasure below, or whether the party even notices the droppings falling from above. The circle within which the birds sit is almost too obvious a metaphor—life, seasons turning, death, onward over one hundred and thirty million years for birds.

Of course, these kestrels aren't closely related to the red-shouldered hawks (*falconiformes* vs. *accipiturs*), but they are still interesting to think about and compare. Baker's peregrines aren't closely related either. These are all very different birds. *Kestrel's Eye* really convinces you that the bird world is out there, penetrating ours but not overshadowing it. That's what I want to capture too.

16 December. Arctic air roaring in. Five days until winter. Autumn holds out with a few green sprigs in sheltered patches, a hopeful delusion. The seasonal cycle spins. The summer shorts and tees go deep into storage. The high today is only forty. I heard a red-shouldered hawk this morning west of the house in the bottoms, but today was one for the scavengers. Driving back home at noon I noticed that the colony of wintering black and turkey vultures had returned, regular as Christmas.

The vultures roost on a new concrete cell tower almost a mile north of the house on the highest fold of the ridge. The tower is a skinny finger of high-tech infrastructure thrust against the red-clay reaches. Not so long ago, maybe fifty years, peach trees spiked the former fields. But for forty years the eastside suburbs have been thick between here and there, sheltering the lives of at least two generations of middle-class communicants in the modern way.

The vultures slump and loiter on every cross piece at the top of the cell tower. I've seen them up there every winter for years. Before colonizing this new cell tower they peppered the thick oaks between the midcentury moderns. Now they prefer the high-up stanchions and spars supporting the cell antennas to rustic oak limbs. I'm sure they prefer the view too, a penthouse perch.

Undeterred by the surrounding houses, the black birds circle and drift in every direction. The outer bands of their circling reach all the way down to our creek, a mile away, and then they ride the thermals up and drift back north to the transmission tower. I counted more than fifty sitting or gliding as I drove by today.

When the visiting vultures gang up, they're called "community groups," and I find this funny considering how freaked out some of my neighbors up the ridge get when the gregarious birds show up each winter. I may be the only local who calls these birds neighbors. I value them for what today is called "ecosystems services," but maybe my neighbors only think of resale value. What if someone notices the loitering posse of buzzards in their backyards, shadowing every winter routine?

The vultures are so quiet when they pass overhead. I look up from the deck and one drifts just above the oak tops. Small adjustments to wing placement cantilever its flight path. A wing tips up, like an acknowledgement from a Blue Angel in formation.

Their patience is palpable, but maybe they're already groggy with the invading cold. I've read they lower their body temperature at night, plunging toward hyperthermia. The wind is in their faces today, roaring out of the north like a southbound freight train. They'll wait it out.

18 December. I will begin in January searching the hawk home territory for last year's nest sites. I will need to do that by foot, and will have to eliminate the areas, one by one. It's exciting to have a first draft of this project almost halfway done. I think back six months to when I read Baker's *The*

Peregrine and I'm struck by how much I have in common with his "watcher," how much I still want to apply Baker's precision of observation and the poetic denseness of prose to my own landscape. I think back to that first hawk nest in our yard and how I now have fifteen years of experience with our neighborhood hawks. I walk out to observe and listen to them. I have faith that a story will find me if pay attention.

19 December. Midday and quite chilly. The Christmas bird count is in progress in the upcountry. All over the region birders tally the local avian populations. My friend Drew has been at it for twenty-two years straight. His day started at five a.m. at a Waffle House eating fried eggs and sausage. I know this because of social media. His Facebook post blew up with requests to join him for a long day of observation in the name of natural history and he has morphed into a Pied Piper. I imagine a caravan of birders carving up territory, communing with the widely scattered feathered wild. These probes of the world that surround us explain so much—what's "out there" beyond our narrow peephole. When I was a child my aunt had what was called a "picture window," and I remember the world always looked so wide and mysterious looking through it.

This morning I saw a black sea of shiny-winged grackles settling under the feeder. Were they refugees from the northern cold? I counted them but lost track quickly—forty, seventy, a hundred? They were a train wreck of particularity, too numerous to quantify. The best I could do was turn the yard into a journal. I took notes and spun out figures of speech. I tapped out similes. Like crepe scraps. Like burnt bacon. Like sooty hinges.

If it's anything like my backyard out there in the world, it's a perfect day for a bird count. Birds are everywhere—the regulars, a few titmice, a tumble of chickadees, a bright bluebird, a pileated woodpecker, an annoyed flicker, a solitary downy on the suet cage, and these hundred black grackles needling in the leaves.

I watch with an intensity I have usually reserved only for the hawks. In the woods the lanky grackles forage, turning leaves. Their beaks are little pickaxes, the leaves, ore they mine for insects. When the whistling grackles take flight, their wings roar. They are a symphony of sounds, a concert performed by sets of scissors opening and closing. Offended by my attention, the grackles flee to the trees. When I settle on the backyard bench and they drift back in, their cries sharp as blades, they skirmish with foraging songbirds. The space is a kettle full of their voices. They are like an invading squad of Darth Vaders.

21 December. Solstice. No hawks. Only a dead gray squirrel in the road being pecked at by the neighborhood crows.

Winter

22 December. The season's first sighting of a red-shouldered hawk. It sits on a low perch in the maple in front of the woodshed. Mousing? The surprise of my approach prompts it to fly. It opens its broad striped tail like a geisha fan.

25 December. Smoking a Christmas brisket in the yard. I hear a red-shouldered calling to the northeast. It is somewhere high in the trees in front of my neighbors' house, maybe fifty yards away. The bird calls three times then goes silent.

4:00 p.m. Warm today and we have all the doors open, a December gift of heat on a planet stressed by climate change. For Christmas Betsy bought me a green spotting scope. I can't quite twist the distant hawks into tight focus, so I look through the wrong end, focus the scope on my own field marks. My skin is pale and a bushy beard covers any lateral throat stripes, auriculars, nape, malar, and lower mandible I might display. My breast and belly band are covered by cloth. If there is a heart inside, it is hidden.

December 26. A red-shouldered hawk flies over the backyard then shoots through the woods and settles in a neighbors' oak. It cries six or seven times then far overhead, straight up, I hear the second hawk's answer, shrill, full-throated, but muted by altitude (I have never seen a red-shouldered so high; at first I thought it was a vulture), and then it banks and circles and commits to a controlled, full-speed descent toward where the first bird is sitting. It folds its wings, picks up more speed, and then pulls up like a gymnast sticking a landing, and drops onto the limb beside the first. It may be a little premature, but I hope this is one of the beginning steps in a red-shouldered courting dance. Maybe the yearly renewals of nuptials are under way, and I will be granted an invitation for the ritual pairing.

27 December. Sitting on the deck midday, unseasonably warm, sixty degrees, wispy trains of cumulus blowing southwest to northeast, I hear the long keeeeer of a red-tailed hawk overhead, and look up to see, almost hovering, a young hawk, flaps out, cinnamon tail fanned, broad wings purchasing, holding, skidding to a stop, then disappearing, beating upwind to the west, and minutes later shooting past to the east, letting loose, gliding over treetops, with all the stops pulled, hurtling with the warm southerly December wind until out of sight.

29 December. Midafternoon. Overcast. A layered drift of vultures above to the north. But I'm surprised by a red-shouldered hawk alertly sitting on the woodshed when I drive in from school. The hawks seem to be moving closer and closer to my own habitual perches, the house, the porch. I seem to be conjuring them. Then, one pulse of its wings and it's gone into the woods.

4 January. My first hawk of the new year was a complete surprise. Late afternoon, cool temperatures (winter weather moving in), I drove a friend down near the entrance to our subdivision. Sitting just inside the swamp fringe was a red-shouldered hawk. It sat there, sullen, unconcerned. We were only ten feet away.

We sat idling in the truck cab and watched for ten minutes. I'd wondered where the birds had been for the last five days, and finally, here one was, seemingly unconcerned that we were intently watching. Maybe it had been hunkered down since the year changed over. Here this one sat, facing into the breeze, with coppery breast feathers fluffed out as a defense against the chill and what seems its frosty mood.

5 January. Every day now adds to a deepening stock of images of the hawks. I walk the dog, try to stay moving. There are standing stale puddles from last week's rain. I walk west to check out yesterday's perch. No hawk there. The skies are empty too. No hawk there either. Today I will have to make do with the Chickadees and wrens, which are active in the privet.

Then, on the northwestern horizon, I hear the birds first, a distant kee-ah kee-ah. I walk toward the sound and look up and see two red-shouldered hawks—as if they are dog-fighting, dipping and looping above the bare oaks, spiraling flecks of dark in the light gaps between the filigree of winter limbs. One hawk hovers there high above the brick split-levels. Are these the first tag-team nuptials for our birds? Just a little spirited aerial display? Time will tell whether mating season is close at hand.

6 January. I circle northeast of our house this morning, scouting for the hawk nest. I bushwhack up a little creek almost to the dam at the lake in the next subdivision east. I start out in the big floodplain that yawns below us but the woods turn dry, thin, and rocky the closer I get to the dam. There are no trails, no signs that anyone ever walks here. The woods have been thinned of timber and are now mostly smaller hardwoods, thirty or forty feet tall. It's chilly, cloudy, and still. There is a feeling of what's to come tonight—a rare snowstorm—a sense everything is seeking shelter. Can the birds sense snow in the air? My mother always talked of "snow birds," and so I look at each passing bird and wonder if these birds are the ones my mother meant.

Once I'm on the higher slopes I see what I think could be a nest high in a forked, thin white oak, but the moment I turn my binoculars to the canopy I scare up two red-tails. Maybe they nest here? The two birds both whistle and circle back to check me out.

Crows and titmice are abundant in the hollies, but no red-shouldered hawks, so I keep walking, getting closer to our neighbors' backyards. Then I chance upon a secret site of teenage anguish and/or agitated solitude, a dry rocky spot overlooking the creek where someone has ripped up a stashed journal and strewn the pieces. I don't look at the pages, reserving a little privacy for the one who had abandoned the journal here. (I write as I walk along, but will carry my pages back with me.)

I continue to walk up the creek. I didn't know there was such topography on the backside of our neighborhood, or how close the dam was to us. The hawks' nest is going to be hard to find.

7 January. I went back to our side yard, where I had observed the nest years before. I looked up in the same oak and in the crotch I spotted a jumble of sticks I'd not seen before. The possibility of a red-shouldered nest AND IT IS IN OUR SIDE YARD AND LESS THAN ONE HUNDRED FEET FROM THE SITES OF THE ONLY OTHER TWO NESTS I HAVE CONFIRMATION OF IN FIFTEEN YEARS! Keep an eye on it!

8 January. What is my project? I vowed to respond to these neighbor birds wherever I see them or hear them. I want my observations to be more than fascination, and I don't want them to be seen as misanthropic, a claim made about Baker's peregrine observations. Baker claimed he wanted to let the human taint wash away in emptiness and silence. Where is the human taint on these birds or their territory? They, like coyotes, do just fine with us around. These hawks are citizens of this republic of subdivisions.

9 January. Two days ago there was no snow. Instead an inch of sleet shellacked the roads and yards. But now it's snow and sleeting again. The click of ice on ice meets the rising sun. All through the morning a sporadic half inch of snow fell, softening the glassy sheen of the yard. Our neighbors are duck hunting—shotguns open up to the southwest, a volley of muted blasts and then silence.

I dreamed last night of the red-shouldered hawks, a frantic scene with crows and hawks in the trees of our front yard. I was trying to get into position to photograph the hawks. There was one hawk in particular I got a clear angle on. I could see the rusty cinnamon-colored feathers of its white-spackled breast. It was perched on a limb. The field guides talk about the hawks' "light crescent windows on the outer wings." I need to look for that. What can I see through those windows?

10 January. Everything is still rare ice and deep Arctic chill—the third day in a row below freezing. I go to the front door and look north, and surprise myself, track the shadow of a hawk, headed west above the splintered trees. The weather hasn't wet the world's fuse. A red-shouldered's cry goes off like a skyrocket. I have been on this quest for seven months, but it wasn't until today that I achieved what I would call a small degree of intimacy with the neighborhood hawks. By two p.m. the temperatures had reached fifty degrees and I went out to try and clear the remaining ice on the sheltered north side of the house. Stepping out the back door, I startled one of the red-shouldered hawks on the ground in the front yard. It was like a dozen other encounters I had had and could have ended there—hawk sighting, then a wing flap, glide, and disappearance into the trees. But this time the bird landed on a low perch in a short poplar at the head of our drive, and I walked up just to just see how close I could get before it flew (it always flew). It didn't fly. I watched and it watched me, its head turned almost entirely around. It shook, preened, lifted one yellow foot then the other, but mostly it scanned the verge around the cul-de-sac where the ice had melted down to the winter-matted leaves. It didn't seem concerned that I was there. I saw the bird's eyes clearly and even speculated about what it was thinking, like a teenager flirting with his crush across a high school library.

My attention had attached me to the hawk and I swear the hawk seemed attached to me as well. And then it flew, but not far, choosing a perch on the white oak at the intersection of the cul-de-sac and the street, a little higher up, to catch more of the winter sun. It was then that I went inside to get my binoculars, fully expecting the bird to be gone when I returned, but no, when I approached the tree, the hawk remained. And then the second hawk came in to perch as well. I realized that one was smaller than the other. Seen that close together for the first time, the size difference was obvious. When the smaller bird saw me it flew into the thicket of brushy oaks on the vacant lot across the street. The larger bird, the one still perched, the one I had flirted with, was clearly the female. And the male was the skittish, untrusting one.

—*I watch you for a ten full minutes. You preen but mostly sit—collapsed into your hawk life with no concern for me. But you let me watch and do not fly. You seem to sense that I'm watching. Then you drop from your perch. There's something in the verge across the road. You kick a little among the leaves and return to your perch with some winter morsel. I watch another ten minutes, because I can, and not much happens. Vultures drift overhead. I hear your mate up the hill calling. Someone runs a chainsaw one street further down. The mailman drives past, curious as to what he cannot see that I am seeing. Finally, you drop again and come up empty, and you move on to another branch. One of the secrets of intimacy is establishing closeness, and today I got there.*

11 January. Midafternoon and I walk out the back door. The female hawk is hanging out behind the truck on an old dogwood tree. She sees me and makes a short flight to a nearby sourwood bent over our walk and looks back. She seems calm so I take a few steps closer. We look at each other and I lean against the truck. The soundscape is drip water off the roof, as it is sixty degrees. The ice is almost gone from everywhere but the shaded north. Five minutes pass and we size each other up. We are practically friends now. Two days in a row we've met and exchanged furtive glances. Well, furtive on my part at least. Then from the side yard, the smaller bird flies in to join her and perches a few feet away in the water oak. It occurs to me for the first time this smaller bird could be a yearling and not her mate at all, still hanging around Mama. What makes me speculate is that I get a good enough look this time to notice that its tail feathers don't seem so fully developed, and it's only half the female's size.

Soon the female is bored with my flirtations and takes the high road, exiting through the trees to the north. The smaller bird follows, vocalizing, the calls retreating through the winter woods.

12 January. Cracklingly bright winter morning and I'm driving west out past the beaver ponds, and against the rising sun I see the silhouette of the larger red-shouldered hawk. It sits on a crossing branch between two slender dead trunks, surveying the marsh. The smaller hawk sits below in more brush, as has often been the case when I have seen them together. The two hawks are a quarter mile from the neighborhood. The larger hawk seems unconcerned with my attention. When I get out of the truck to photograph her, the smaller hawk takes off. He doesn't react well when I stop. He always leaves the scene.

13 January. Another warm winter morning at the beaver ponds and another hawk sighting. The large female sits calmly on a broken-off tree next to the outlet creek. It is as if she is sitting on the end of a telephone pole. The smaller bird perches nearby, lower down. They now hang out in this area every morning. I whistle a couple of times. She looks at me and is unconcerned by my intrusion. Before I can get a photograph, she drops, skims the matted grass below, then flies off at a low angle. I do not see whether she catches something or not.

Later. Everything is active—hearing two pileated woodpeckers in the woods below me right now.

14 January. It is through sound I keep up with them. In the warm months it was easy, their cries went off like air raid sirens. But they seem to be less noisy now. I've been wondering about their hanging out at the beaver ponds. Is that visitation seasonal? Does that location offer better hunting in the winter than the road verges? All of life depends on shopping for food. When I muse about the habits of the hawks, a friend writes, "Every day is a beginning WHEN YOU ARE A HAWK. Waking to hunger. The same hunger, only this time it's fresh. And new. And now. And yours."

But there is something beyond hunger. I have watched the bigger female hawk closely, sometimes for as long as fifteen minutes, as she sat on a low perch. At those times she kept an eye on me as well. It may simply be habituation—I have had more time to pursue and locate the hawks since Christmas. Of course, I would like it to be affectionate familiarity, the recognition of individual faces that researchers have clearly attributed to crows. Though I would like this, I will withhold judgment, remembering what J. A. Baker warned in *The Peregrine*, that the human shape may be hostile to a bird of prey, but that over time it is possible, but difficult, to sink into "the skin and bones of a hawk" and know it. It took Baker ten years of close observation.

4:00 p.m. Betsy and I walked with the dog all the way to the beaver ponds, to see if the hawks were hanging out there today. Before we arrived, high on the ridge near a tall windrow of planted loblollies in the outward line of houses in our subdivision, I heard a red-shouldered hawk crying four or five times, then in a closer oak heard another hawk on a lower perch. I turned my binoculars toward the faraway pines but couldn't locate either bird. I was back to my "sound-only" observations. Walking further west we reached the end of the road, where the beaver ponds intersect it, and we turned around. I heard a wood duck in the wetland, and I saw cardinals, a mockingbird, and a single sparrow foraging in old blackberry cane along the wet margin.

When we turned back east to head home I finally saw the smaller hawk take off and fly southwest over the duck pond and the creek. I saw clearly by its speed and the length of its tail that it was not the smaller red-shouldered hawk after all, but a Cooper's hawk intent on some distant destination.

15 January. Days of unseasonable warmth. I heard one of the red-shouldered hawks to the west in the swamp-forest and went out to find it. Four calls. It was perched somewhere in the winter trees. I walked the trail west and heard it again—two calls this time. Then I walked to the foot of the subdivision road and it cried one more time—one, two, three, four again—and broke cover, flying south through the trees. It looked like the small hawk and retreated noisily toward the river. Off to the north I heard an answering call—the female. As I walked I thought back to the film *Kestrel's Eye* and the idea of "life below." I was walking through the bird world. A jogger appeared and disappeared, her ears stoppered against the sounds I craved. A car started and my neighbors went off, probably to church.

As I wandered on down the street out of the subdivision, some neighbors came out and asked with a smile, "What are you doing at the foot of our drive?" I told them I was watching the neighborhood hawks, and they seemed mildly interested and vaguely intrigued, so I told them about my project, including my reading of *The Peregrine*. "They're always around," the wife said. "They nest right up there." She pointed up the hill beside their house. I scanned the trees and thought, maybe I've missed an obvious nest, but all I could see were some messy squirrel nests.

I walked on to the beaver ponds and the crows certified my approach with exchanges. Both hawks were there, as if waiting for me. And the whole troupe of vultures that a month earlier had been roosting on the tall cell tower up the hill has moved down into the bottoms closer to us. They were completely spread out, sunning, thermoregulating, on snags and crossbars. Along the high-tension right-of-way between the duck pond and the beaver ponds, the vultures have now commandeered a transmission tower. They sat side by side on steel cross pieces, thirty birds positioned on each one. The bulk of the dark resident troupe was bivouacked in the copse of red oaks along the far ridge. A hundred vultures sat on a dozen large leafless trees. When I looked up there were others returning from outward scavenging forays, almost as dramatic as the winged monkeys returning to Oz.

16 January. Overcast day. Walked out the front door and right into a mixed flock of cedar waxwings and robins foraging in the middle distances of the canopy, mostly on dried sourwood blooms. Dozens of birds. Later at the gate to the duck pond I spotted a wild turkey and five black vultures on the ground. Just a moment later I heard the red-shouldered hawk cry three times to my west but never spotted it. There were crows at the beaver ponds, and about ten vultures still roosting, part of yesterday's congress. Small shoals of foraging songbirds swept from side to side on the little spillway slough, and the traffic on the road was heavy. That time of day it was mostly lawn crews moving around in trucks, hauling trailers, keeping up with the "blowing and mowing" even though it was winter. Then I heard the hawk again, and then—were those chorus frogs? Two vultures flew over, flapping so hard I thought at first they were the hawks. The red-shouldered hawk was perched somewhere out there before me, sheltered from my gaze by the thick vegetation of the watery wastes.

17 January. 11:00 a.m. Fifty-seven degrees. Chorus frogs thrum in the beaver ponds. Like a throng of fifties greasers strumming their plastic combs in unison. The warm weather has nudged them from their winter slumber. The crows aren't happy that this other order (the frogs) gets all the attention—a group of crows watches my parked vehicle and adds an insult or two.

4:00 p.m. I walk back to record the frogs. They are at full tilt and I get eighteen seconds of clicking, a metallic surge, a hallelujah chorus hidden in the dormant seedy cattails. But mostly the beaver ponds are a disappointment compared to earlier in the day. Not even the persistent crowd of crows hassles the visitor with the strange black eyes. A sheet of silence settles over everything, save the frogs. Nothing's stopping them.

On the way back, though, a red-shouldered hawk appears when I am almost home. It comes in high from the southwest, settles in a tree in a yard, and lets out a three screams, as if to say to me, "I've been watching too and now here I am." I whistle three times, as shrill as my voice will go. In answer, she takes off and flies, as if on a mission, due east.

20 January. Rain. Irregular torrents, then long pauses, and a steady drip as it drains through the trees. Dark still, and it will be for hours. I am in a dark dawn Inauguration Day mood.

Two days ago I took students from a wildlife-tracking class hiking at the old mill site a mile downstream. As we got started, a red-shouldered hawk powered overhead with something in its talons, landed in a streamside snag, and put on a little locavore show above us—ripping flaccid strips of fresh meat from a long flimsy tube, a January snake harvested from a sunny spot. The feasting hawk was soon joined by another. This must be the next home territory downstream, the foraging neighbors of our hawks.

We left the public trail, bushwhacked a quarter mile along the stream bank to the confluence with a smaller creek where I had never been. There on a sandbar the students found a fan of dark gray feathers and the freshly gnawed bones and sinews of a great blue heron. One primary feather floated on the stream. In this lonely spot an ambush had occurred—likely a bobcat, as the students pointed out that the bird had been plucked, and that's a sign of a cat kill, according to their animal signs field guide.

The next day, while driving in town I saw the crumpled disheveled carcass of a large red-tailed hawk in the verge of the street in front of my bank. If you're a hawk, January is not a bad month to collide with a car, as there are no eggs to incubate or nestlings to feed. No one has been abandoned. It will be long season for a mate. Maybe a year from now a young dispersing hawk will inherit an unexpected territory.

I recount these three somber events in the natural world around me, unrecorded until now, because that's how I'm feeling this day. Someday we will all be ambushed by history and collide with the future.

Noon. And then as if to lift my spirits, I'm driving home, down through the center of the suburb, and I can't believe it but sitting on a mailbox on my side of the road is a red-shouldered hawk. Is it one of ours?

I whip the truck around and stop to observe. The bird seems darker, almost chocolate brown. I'm north of the house, maybe a half mile, so it may very well be the hawk I have seen perched above the retention pond at the patio development up along the main road. The bird drops into a mulch island in the center of the lawn and thrashes its beak back and forth and eats something, then does it again. Worms or a small snake maybe, out on a warm January day? Baker said that he observed peregrines eating earthworms, and it raised doubt among the experts about his narrative since such feeding had never been reported in the official literature. I'm not an expert, but my observations pile up day to day, and I know that if I watch something long enough I may see something new. As apologists for Baker often note, there is plenty of mystery left in nature.

21 January. I'm standing outside the screen porch on the deck, sullen after scanning the news cycle online. A crow skirmish erupts to the south next to the river. Then I hear it—the red-shouldered hawk crying from the middle of the scrum. One cry, and then silence for a split second. Immediately crows tune up again, capable of no such pause, their caws bouncing between the winter trees. The misting rain tamps down the hullabaloo. I'm wearing a light jacket against the rain. A large patrol of cardinals takes a turn at the tube feeder. They retreat, perch in the yaupon holly, and then drop to the birdbath like hang gliding insurgents.

I go back into the porch. Two Carolina wrens feel agonistic as well; they skirmish to within a few feet of where I sit down in the glider, then call a truce to sit side by side on a deck chairback and eyeball the watcher, weighing their options across the no-man's-land between us.

Yesterday's inauguration has brought on this eruption of war metaphors and similes of strife. Maybe I have dropped into Trumpland by osmosis. Everything becomes a battle, a deal, a face-off of winners and losers, the old tooth and claw. The crows have moved downstream. The hawk disappears, the moment closing like a hinge. I close-read the yard like an

English professor, open my tablet, and tap my crude cuneiform to capture it all. And then I focus on the wren, which has now returned, beak-needling the falling leaves under the table. It's always lunchtime in wrenland, hawkland, crowland, and the kingdom of cardinals.

23 January. Warm enough for frog calls. A steady wind from the west pushing out the last of the gunmetal clouds of yesterday. The sky now is baby blue at the horizon and cerulean where the bowl curves. Directly overhead the resident colony of turkey vultures wheels and teeters, flashing the white of their wings' undersides. At first they gang and gyre together on the thermal, then they splinter into smaller drifts of black wrinkles, and sink a hundred feet in an instant, headed toward their roost.

A red-shouldered hawk's brief appearance distracts me. One of the birds beelines from west to east over the bottoms at canopy height. Four calls. I watch it minutes later—a flash of breast glowing tangerine—working back along the creek, from perch to perch.

24 January. Near dawn. The temperature is fifty-four degrees, like a spring morning, and when I put out the dog I hear chorus frogs singing their mass metallic love ballad in the bottoms. Did they sing through the night, a Woodstock of frog song? Do they chart more than temperature? Can they sense the barometer falling slowly as a warm front drifts through from the southwest? They say we get our weather from Atlanta, and this morning they've sent us warm rain, a frog's paradise.

Far enough away, competing with the wind chimes, the frogs sound now like sleigh bells or someone's steady hand shaking a jar of steel shavings, a drum machine's ponderous rhythm track. Is this the winter of love, or is it still weeks distant and this only a tune-up, a one-night stand? Is that yearly orgy right around the corner in this warming world?

Though frogs are on my mind, I've been up thinking about vultures, trying to understand lift and the dynamics of local thermals. I've laid out government maps and drawn vector currents with pink and blue pens, masses sweeping up our surrounding ridges like tides, air instead of water, generated by the sun, not the moon. I've always known that the southern piedmont landscape is a crumpled sheet on a tilted tabletop and we live in one of the deep wrinkles. What I've considered less is how terrain affects the habits of birds. I've located "ridge lift" and deciphered the fingerprint intricacy of the topo lines around us. I've noted that the high ridges are fifty meters above the creek. They go high because the creek runs low.

I'm exploring thermals and lift because yesterday, when I could find no hawks, I instead watched a colony of vultures clotting the sky above the high ridge where they roost. I counted seventy-one vultures, mostly turkey but a few black, launching off the cell tower there into the warming morning air, soaring up to the ridge's apex in spirals, intent on rising.

Concerned texts have come in from a neighbor who'd looked skyward and thought of Alfred Hitchcock, seeing the soaring black birds as a nightmare in the making. "What is up with all those buzzards flying around?" she wrote. I tried to explain my fascination, help her become enchanted with our colony of wintering raptors. I called the white undersides of their wings flashing in the sun "beautiful." She wrote back, "You say beautiful, I say creepy."

All day the vultures climbed and drifted. In spite of neighboring ideas of a horror show, I checked the sky every couple of hours until the birds reached their own apex and spiraled down. By evening a relaxed patrol glided just over the treetops along the creek, the lowest point on the map, the springhead of liftoff for currents. At dusk they were all gone, likely gathered back at their roosts—dead trees in the swamp and the high perches offered by the tall transmission tower.

7:45 a.m. One of the red-shouldered hawks calls to me from a tall oak near the river to the southeast, as if to chide me for paying so much attention to the vultures. When I go out on the deck the bird takes off from the high perch and bullets east into morning. I hear it move like an invisible curser over the screen of pinks, whites, and baby blues of the rising sun. Then to the northeast, I hear the second bird, what Robert Frost might call "copy-speech . . . counter-love, original response," winging in for rendezvous.

25 January. A friend writes with two great questions about the vultures—"Do they think we built the towers for them? And will they get cancer?" He also mentioned his own "vulture/thermal fascinations," and where they had led through the years—particularly to discussions with a friend who pilots a small plane and how through these conversations he had begun to imagine a "landscape over the landscape."

My friend's questions about the vultures and about cancer lead me to the Internet. Who knows? Scientific research is a vast landscape, and maybe someone out there has tested the health of roosting vultures.

The first interesting hit is a scientific paper that contains two of the three search terms—"vultures" and "cell-phone towers." I like the absurdity of the language in peer-review science papers—"taxidermic effigies," "problem-roost situations."

I know that neither of my friend's vulture questions can be answered. As for the first question, how would we set up an experiment to determine whether or not the vultures think the towers were built for them? The second question, I guess, could be answered through experiment, but it would take a cancer researcher to set it up. Out of my friend's questions came some of my own: How far do these seventy-one local cell tower vultures disperse in the warmer months? Do these the birds make up the half the vulture population of the county or are they out-of-state vultures that migrate south a state or two in fall and up a state or two in spring?

26 January. The vultures have hijacked the neighborhood. Late afternoon I walked the dog a half mile west to the beaver ponds. Along the way a clutch of the silent wheeling birds shadowed my stride. A vulture shadow is dense. It blacklists the ground under it. These birds are cobalt crosses, moving dungeons cast from above. I watched the vultures play the currents, shifting back and forth like noiseless fighter planes in haphazard formation, steep banks followed by flat glides.

Walking down to the beaver ponds I saw two dozen vulture congregants weighing down a large dead oak, black fruit slumped on sloughing boughs.

Is this the winter vulture apex? Is this why they have shifted from the cell tower on the ridge to the two transmission towers in the lowlands? Will their ranks swell even more before the next phase—their departure to mate and nest somewhere, raising young? They don't actually build nests, instead laying their large eggs directly on the ground, often in caves, hollow trees, abandoned buildings, and even stumps. Like our neighborhood hawks, vulture pairs may also return to successful sites for years in a row, so their fierce loyalty to place helps account for their presence every winter in our neighborhood. For now they prefer the forest of drowned trees in the beaver ponds to the cell tower up on the main road.

27 January. 7:30 a.m. Just as the sky bleeds from deep black to milky blue, the hawks cry. Walking out to get the paper I hear the piercing song of the red-shouldereds calling each to each from the west, a set of screeching hiccups, somewhere between me and the two hundred silent roosting vultures. And as if to assure me how complex the neighborhood really is, shotguns let loose on the duck pond—a dozen rounds booming death from below.

28 January. This morning I swear the air smells like goose shit, and, as if on cue, scattered geese call from the killing ground at the duck pond, crows sound alarm, and then the whole neighborhood goes silent again. Soon after I walk the half mile on the road to the beaver ponds to see what effect the duck and goose hunting has had on the bedded-down battalion of vultures, and as I approach the wetlands the cinnamon breast of one of the red-shouldered hawks crosses above me, lit up like a lantern by the early light from the east, a spear-flight from tree line to tree line, followed by the usual screaming introduction—ker-yeer, ker-yeer, keeer-yeer!

On the transmission tower, vultures hop, vault, bound, and jounce on the steel supports with each barrage from the nearby duck pond. One bird circles tensely, tightening a noose of air.

The hawk can't settle down, hops snag to snag toward the slumped horde of vultures on the ridgeline, calling all the way. In the brush, the drifts of winter bramble, small mixed flocks of songbirds flit in and out of the frosty canes—cardinals, robins, wrens, and one nervous mockingbird. A great blue heron huddles tensely on a stump, and three peeting wood ducks beat at the open water of the narrow drainage ditch to take flight.

The hawk won't settle down long enough for me to get my binoculars on it, and I follow farther west than ever before across the busy road and onto the trashy shoulder there. I get a glimpse of the hawk advancing into the first lines of the settled turkey vultures attentive on the ridge. As the hawk sits among them, the vultures take offense and retreat until a new wave of ten black vultures gliding in from the direction of the shooting tips the balance, and clots the landing zone.

The hawk's had it, maybe with the gunfire, the vultures, or the watcher stalking from below, and beelines for the east, directly into the rising sun.

29 January. The vultures soar over our house and I feel a deep transspecies connection—a window into the origins of freedom, wildness, and old behavioral patterns, all playing out above me. This is the opposite of shadowing. This is buzzard life flaring in the sun, an avian firework display, a silver tonic to a week's darkness. What's pulling them to our neighborhood? Is it some old homing instinct that goes back much longer than our suburb? Why do they wobble through their orbits like bent rims?

30 January. I drive to the beaver ponds to check in, to inventory the black tents of vulture bodies slumped against the cold on bare limbs and steel stanchions, as they had been yesterday, and they are all gone. In just twelve hours, as if some order came to ship out, they've all vanished. Poof. Adios. The ponds are silent.

Only a lone great blue heron stands watch until I stop the truck and point my binoculars at the trees. Alone on a limb that the day before had been thick with roosting vultures I see the fluffed-out cinnamon-breasted red-shouldered hawk, staring toward the duck pond. Hunched against the breeze, she swivels her head, notes my interest, and turns back to her survey.

It's dangerous to project human emotions on a bird, but she looks lonely, sullen, and abandoned. Where is the smaller hawk I saw her with last week? Was it a transient who scored some hospitality in the neighborhood, or one of last year's chicks that has now dispersed into the larger world, ready to confront the hard arithmetic of hawk reality, who survives and who doesn't. These are the thoughts I project on the hawk as I watch from the road. Then my thoughts and emotions turn to feeding. Is there in her hawk head a trigger latch set for when to stoop on some morsel exposed below?

1 February. A month into winter now but spring will soon approach. I am fretful again about finding the nest, about what the rest of the year will hold. Will the hawks nest? Will I find it? Will it be in some spot I can observe it without disturbing the nesting or trespassing? If I don't have a nest, do I still have a story? I need to be patient and trust that the year will unfold, and will round into what it will be, and it will work.

I stay the course. My story is unfolding day to day. Just before dusk, a chilly foreboding wind in my face, I walk to the beaver ponds for some relief, to record peeting wood ducks, to see the sullen vultures (one hundred and thirty this time) huddled on the transmission tower and the nearby dark trees. For the first time in a week there are no hawks but in spite of that they remain my most hopeful idea, a promise, wherever they're settled in.

2 February. Midday I head to school. A warm wind from the southwest allows me to drive with the windows down. I stop on a tight curve of Snake Road where I hear a red-shouldered hawk's welcome cry from the nearby beaver ponds. In a swaying pencil of a distant tree sits the precarious hawk, backlit, blowing in the breeze like a blank flag. With the binoculars I amplify my view, and the cinnamon breast feathers ruffle in the steady wind. It's the short-tailed smaller bird. He sways there and doesn't retreat, hanging on to a branch at an odd angle off the thin main trunk. I whistle my bad hawk intimation—three rounds, then three more. No response. The bird almost looks offended and turns away.

Above the hawk gyre seven vultures. Breeze-drunk, they stumble through abrupt turns and banks, like bumper cars avoiding collision in the whimsy of the warm wind. The sky is creamy blue behind them, and cirrus clouds—crinoids, wispy mare's tails—form icy curls at high altitude.

The wetland sits silent, though sometimes the wind rattles the remaining leaves and gossips in the grass. Even the hopping flights of small birds, common in the brambles, ceases. Where do these rafts of birds moor? Only the hawk and the vultures, biding time in the breeze, animate the day.

7:00 p.m. Dusk. We walked the dog to the beaver ponds. My wife power walked ahead and I meandered slowly with the listless overweight beagle as he marked every leaf pile to stall the exercise. I saw a few vultures through the trees but couldn't anticipate the shock of the choreography above once I broke clear of forest cover and looked up to see spiraling arms of a vulture galaxy forming and dispersing above. Several hundred birds glided at multiple levels, riding downward and then powering back up to altitude to swirl before descending again.

There was a music to this coasting, but it was a slow, silent score. The lack of sound was actually unnerving, like a stealth invasion, a back-channel occupation, a surreptitious temporary colony arrived from deep space. If these birds had been fireworks Betsy and the dog would have looked up, but since the birds made no sound, only I saw the pyrotechnics. The dog meandered on, oblivious to the show above, more wedded to a stinking pumpkin collapsing in the ditch. When we reunited I pointed up in wonder, and Betsy said, "Oh my, it's a vulture murmuration!"

3 February. Early morning, I drive past the beaver ponds. I block the glare, the sun now a hand's width above the horizon. Blinded by the spreading dawn streaked orange and pink, I pull off onto the shoulder as a red-shouldered hawk screams overhead. Another hawk answers from deep in the wetlands. I fix its silhouette high in a rotting snag against the backdrop of sky banded with clouds. A few dozen dispersing vultures drift in and out of view. I look toward last night's roosting spot in the power right-of-way. Where two hundred had congregated, twenty now loiter on the ground like vagrants.

Out in the ponds the two hawks fly diagonals back and forth, crying all along. Do they dogfight a little? Do they line dance? Could this be pair-bonding? Time, and the advancing spring, will tell. I turn my binoculars on the wetlands once more. The sky is a milky blue, soon to be curdled by the unseasonable heat of the day. For now the hawks retreat and perch, retreat and perch. I listen until their cries recede.

4 February. Dawn. A coal-black smear on the southwest horizon. Two great blue herons balance precariously on a snag in the beaver ponds. One of the red-shouldered hawks sits on a dead tree deeper in the wetlands, a distant black spot, even using binoculars. Chorus frogs celebrate the unseasonal warmth. Geese cry in the distance and sparrows chirp in the brush.

1:00 p.m. I've wondered what this army of resident vultures eats. I drove to meet a friend for breakfast, and on the main road I saw a freshly mashed possum. The guts trailed like prayer flags from the carcass. When I passed again at noon, the road had been cleaned like a plate. All that remained was a greasy stain. Then later still, on the secondary street in a nearby suburb, I slowed for a foraging flock of black vultures blocking traffic, gyrating like helicopters up and down on the pavement, bickering over what seemed a trifle—the remains of something once living. Groundhog? Possum? Unlucky house cat? I watched for five minutes. A dozen vultures took turns, entering from yards on either side, playing dodgeball with a UPS truck and four cars that are forced to slow for this unscheduled episode of *Wild Kingdom*. When I drove back through, the cleanup crew was down to one juvenile ripping at what little remained in the yard.

6:15 p.m. I drove past the beaver pond and power right-of-way on the way home. Not one vulture was to be found. Had they moved on again as they had done twice before? I walked back at dusk and the spring peepers opened up for the first time this year—mainly in the drainage ditches near the duck pond, and the chorus frogs opened up in their little corner of the wetlands. And the vultures were back. Eighty-five roosting on the transmission tower and nearby trees, and ten sitting on the ground in the grass, but the real show was in the air. Thirty or forty birds swung in tight acrobatic circles over the treetops.

5 February. Early morning, chilly and gray, and both hawks cry east of the house, the first time in two weeks I have heard them from that direction. They are on the move. One cries at a normal pace but the other bird is frantic, its cry high-pitched, accompanied, of course, by the caws of pursuing crows. Maybe buteo courting has begun? Sonic foreplay? Preliminary love peeps? Opening pursuit? Who knows? If they are going to bond it has to happen soon.

3:00 p.m. Liftoff. First observation of hawk hanky-panky! About fifty of the voyeur vultures watch from the tower as well. One hawk in the trees to the left comes in crying keer-yee, keer-yee, keer-yee, and lands on a limb. The smaller bird flies in from the right crying in counterpoint and lands in a sweet gum nearby. At first I think, my God they're going to share the same limb! Then the smaller male flies in, lands right on top of larger female! No sound that I can hear. A couple of wingbeats, both birds balanced, more wingbeats, then the smaller male retreats, flies maybe a hundred yards and sits on another snag. It's lasted about five seconds. There are no steep dives by the male, no soaring upward and calling by the female, no "skydance," as the field guides often describes it. The act is brief, ordinary, and strangely tender. I wish I'd been close enough to hear her "utter short cries before, during, and after copulation" as the field guides claim. But no such luck. I watch from the pavement like a Peeping Tom. She does not seem embarrassed though. She sits preening on the branch and looks toward me as her mate retreats up the river.

It's been fifteen minutes since the copulation. After the action the wetland went silent, but now the chorus frogs have let loose. She hears them. How can she not? There is a steady rasping, like thumbs pulled across a hundred combs. Then just as fast, the frogs stop and start up in another part of the wetlands between me and the attentive hawk. She faces me as if to scold. Cars roll past. Sparrows chirp. I look down at my phone and write, "Two big woodpeckers beat past," and while I'm tapping, the female hawk leaves silently.

6 February. How could I not return to the breeding ground? Midmorning I walk back to the beaver ponds. The chorus frogs now sound like a roomful of wooden tumblers clicking into the place. Titmice take short flights through the blowing cotton of cattails. Forty-six degrees. Clear skies. I'm looking directly into the sun, putting temporary blinders on my prurient survey. Finally I focus again, and the sun flare subsides. The vultures are gone. The transmission tower is vacant. Not one vulture in sight. I scan the wetland with my binoculars. To my disappointment, the love-tree, erect and dark, is empty of hawks. They've found another sugar shack. Then I hear it, the call of a single red-shouldered hawk at the duck pond echoing back and forth, back and forth, plaintive and distant. I look deeper into the trees. Too far away to see, the hawk flies in short hops upstream along the creek, then keeps calling, on the move. Is it the female or the male? Whichever, it seems to be looking for love in all the wrong places this morning.

Instead, an avian stand-in, one black vulture, appears, gyrates above the nearby trees in tight circles, and spooks a bluebird, which flies out of the wetlands and nearly right into my face before it veers. There must be others because bluebirds, like ranging teenagers, rarely travel alone.

Then, as if in punctuation to my hope for more salacious sightings, one of the great blue herons drifts in from the north, lands on a snag in the beaver ponds, and honks his horn like Harpo Marx in *Duck Soup*.

Sunset. A hundred vultures occupy the transmission tower and trees around the duck pond again. None soar. I don't know enough about weather to understand why three days ago they twirled and danced on the breezes until the sun set and tonight they sit earthbound, a colony of low expectations.

7 February. Scanning the bottoms from the screened porch, I am titillated when I notice for the first time this year the red-pink mist of maple flower clusters appearing well before the less romantic leaves emerge. The flowers flare and float, hot spots in the drowned winter forest, pale fire, like afterimages of flame through cloudy glass.

Botanists say the red maple flowers are unisexual, some male, some female, but under the right conditions the maple can switch from male to female, male to hermaphroditic, and hermaphroditic to female. The hawks have sex lives that fit more neatly in either/or boxes. Though generally monogamous, one researcher recorded a "trio," a female initiating threesomes, soliciting sex from multiple males in adjacent territories.

Red maple, which thrives in wet soil, is an indicator species for the moisture-loving red-shouldered hawks I chase. Maybe by flying the birds acquire some sort of sympathetic pigment acquisition, the red of maples bleeding into the wings and breast of the hawks as they pass through on their daily rounds. A permanent stain.

The hawks have made me a loafer and I'm comfortable in my midday leisure on the porch. More and more my days are lost to following their calls.

Like earlier today, when I headed home early for lunch with the excuse of finishing my syllabus, and instead of turning onto our street I paused on the edge of the beaver ponds, parked my truck, and stepped out into my own high drama. Listening for the hawks is my excuse, but don't discount the zombie presence of J. A. Baker—dead now forty years—that pulls me out into the fresh air more and more. Now deep in my own project, I think of Baker at the oddest times—recalling images from *The Peregrine*: seeing Baker bent over his bicycle peddling up a lane, or Baker staying up late to fill in his notes with a tight, strict script. I marvel at his ten-year project and I also marvel at my own luck. His book is about one third frozen tundra—all sun, snow, and blood, his primary colors. I got the other side of the great wheel—not only the death but the sex as well.

As I stood near the ponds listening, up the hill, as if I'd conjured it—kerr-ye, kerr-ye, kerr-ye—a hawk screamed, moving north along the big road. And then I noticed a hawk cruising above me, higher than I'd seen the red-shouldered hawk before. It carved several long loops like a vulture, then dropped like a stone into the woods along the duck pond. Was it one of our birds or an interloper? It cruised through the same quadrant of sky above where I first saw the two birds romancing two days ago. But I couldn't get a good view. This hawk seemed larger than either of the neighborhood hawks. Was it a red-tailed hawk, or another species passing through? I watched for a few minutes but the hawk never reappeared and never cried.

As I drove north my questions were answered. The neighborhood hawks cavorted in a red maple at the corner of our subdivision entrance, on the edge of the swamp-forest.

I jumped out of the truck with my binoculars in hand, left the vehicle dangerously half on, half off the road, reacted like a young cop on patrol who sees a prowler. But those birds were on the prowl for each other. Just as I jumped out, the female screamed and corkscrewed down through the canopy and landed on a limb fifteen feet off the ground. The male danced above her, then plunged, settling on to her back, and they harmonized for a moment, wings fluttering— one, two, three, four, five!—then broke and cartwheeled up the hill out of the floodplain into a grove of oaks. The female landed on a stout oak limb and sat with her back to me. The male circled overhead, screamed. I watched the female with my binoculars but she didn't move, huddled on the limb, stunned and resting. Then she took off and flew up behind a neighbor's house and I went giddy. She'd landed on a nest! I twisted to focus and still couldn't say for sure if I was right or wrong. Was it a squirrel's nest she was simply sitting on top of to recover from her swoon while her lover hovered overhead and aimed for another plunge? Or was it simply a snarl of sticks and leaves that happened to be in her way when she fled and landed?

8 February. The love story I've been writing, of hawk courtship and consummation, takes a dark turn. I walk the dog to the beaver ponds and rather than our usual route of out and back we take the cut-through street, and when we are close to the subdivision entrance we walk right under the female hawk sitting on a low limb of a post oak. She's ten feet above the road, facing north. We are thirty yards from the big trees where I'd seen the birds copulating earlier.

The hawk isn't spooked at all—she's indifferent and not even curious. She watches the dog as he meanders, leashed and silent, underneath. She is intent to sit and observe, unconcerned by my own curiosity and slowing pace. Her breastplate is brightly lit by the late afternoon sun, no longer cinnamon, verging on rusty red. I admire her for a magic moment of intimacy. It's the closest I've been to her in six months and I'm not about to let this moment pass. Baker often made his observations from far below. His peregrines were often as distant as fighter planes, little specks high in the Essex sky. A close encounter for Baker was thirty yards away. In these moments of intimacy Baker had transformative experiences—once a peregrine circled back and sat in a tree twenty yards away. He described how the hawk's eye did not widen in fear, and he believed that in that moment the hawk finally half accepted him, even considered him half a hawk and half a man. Is this an acceptance moment for me? I don't think so. Her motives are easy to gauge. I have stepped into a story as old as animal life itself. What galvanizes her undivided attention are six fat chickens scratching and foraging among the fescue and monkey grass.

When I get home I Google "red-shouldered hawk chickens" and pull up a video taken with a game cam in a backyard. There's a chicken coop just like the one our neighbors constructed, and the remote video recording begins when the hawk flies in and triggers the motion sensor. The hawk circles the coop, lands on the ground, and sizes up the situation. The hawk slow-hops, expertly probing for entrances. It looks underneath the coop. It hops along the wire fence and looks for a break to reach the hens that must be roosting inside.

A hawk hunting on the ground looks Mesozoic. It's when a raptor looks most reptilian and threatening. Displaying the single-minded, calculating search, the hawk has the prefect tool: the inquisitive eye, the long scissor legs, probing beak. There's nothing reflective about hunting for the hawk. There are no philosophical debates. No good and evil to weigh. Those issues were decided for predators tens of millions of years ago. The video I find of a hawk on the hunt puts all the projections I make onto this situation into context. This—"the bloodiness of killing"—is Baker's primary theme for two hundred pages, and I'd be a fool if I didn't know that sooner or later it would even be mine. No matter how much hawk sex you witness, it's hard to discount the search for the next meal. The hawk in the video gets a notion and flies to the roof of the coop. Watching the hawk calculate confirms what the horror writers know. It's like watching Freddy Krueger searching an abandoned house for the teenager hiding in the closet.

From the coop's roof the hawk hops down into the chicken yard and then bursts into the coop itself. The chickens inside utter startled squawks of distress, and then in rapid-fire, one by one, five fly out and huddle against the wire in the far end of the small yard and go silent. Inside, you hear the one unlucky hen. Though you can't see the process, the hawk likely has the hen in its talons, pinned to the coop's floor. Maybe the lungs are punctured, as that would explain the rasping repetition of the cry. Maybe the hawk pecks from time to time to shorten the process. Whatever the situation, the squawks of the doomed chicken go from constant to a pulse or two of panic, then a pause, two more panicked rasping cries, pause, two more, pause, one more long expulsion, more relaxed, then finally silence in the coop as the video ends. "Here, you see a hawk come in and take out my favorite chicken, a black Wyandotte named Sassypants," the commentary accompanying the video reports. "The video is for informative purposes only. It's not gory, just very sad. I will be making some alterations to my chicken coop soon."

I stand at the fence along the street and watch the chickens foraging between the neighbor's azaleas. Then the neighbor's children bound out the back door into the yard followed by their two noisy dogs. The hawk has had enough and leaves the branch, hurled as if by slingshot through the limbs of thick trees as she disappears.

9 February. Early morning. Very warm and I'm in short sleeves for the first time. The hawks are at it again. The female's high-pitched cries signal her reception. The male moves in. The crows mock from the periphery and zero in from every direction, flying over like a formation of disruptive scythes.

4:00 p.m. On the way home from school I park at the beaver ponds, where a pod of shrouded onlookers—a mixed flock of grounded black and turkey vultures—keep their own counsel on the transmission tower crossbars. It's nice to be focused on the vultures again after three days of hawk drama in the trees. I look up through layers of cavorting birds. The kettle sky boils. Some vultures soar so high that even through binoculars they are only black pepper on a blue tablecloth. Others play chicken with the treetops, pulling up at the last moment to take another wind-assisted lap around the wetlands. Are they playing? Does it just feel good to roll with the wind? Vulture-mind must be full of windy alleys and uplifts. The Wright brothers would understand. The undersides of the turkey vulture wings flash with every adjustment of velocity and angle.

I am so distracted by the vultures above that I nearly miss the male red-shouldered clinging to a pencil-thin sweet gum, facing into the west wind. He looks wasted down to his stubby striped tail. He needs a comb. The feathers on his crown and nape blow in the buffeting breeze. His sweetheart is nowhere to be heard. Is she casing the chickens again? House hunting for her nest site? On rat patrol?

How often do they do it? I've heard their frantic cries twice today in the distant woods behind the house, but figured I should not chronicle every copulation. The field guides claim courtship displays can last eighteen days. No wonder the little guy is tired.

10 February. The woods around the house smelled warm, though soggy, as I drove, windows down, to meet a friend for breakfast. Passing the beaver ponds in the dark I entered a shadowed chiming cove of frogsong. All around was a mix of chorus frogs and spring peepers. I pulled the truck off the road. The near-dawn drainage ditches were a factory with full employment, frogs working overtime, finishing up third shift. The vultures huddled on the tower, and the trees in the wetlands barely tracked against the blue-black sky.

An hour later, when I returned, the light had risen, shutting down the frogs, and a few vultures soaked up the early muted sun in the lowest branches of the trees, but many others strolled aimlessly in the street. I hadn't been so close to vultures before, and I slowed to a crawl and parted their parade.

11 February. Today I showed Werner Herzog's *Grizzly Man* to my students. One of Herzog's primary questions surfaces in this film—where is the line between people and animals we should never cross? What would Herzog make of my wife's comment about my heart going out to the hawks? Should your heart stay true to your own species only? The subject of Herzog's documentary, Timothy Treadwell, had obviously "gone over." He lives and then dies after intimate contact with grizzly bears in the Alaskan backcountry for thirteen summers. Treadwell is not a bear biologist; instead he is a wildlife advocate and "friend" of the bears. He makes the wild bears accessible in his one hundred hours of video (Herzog was given access to Treadwell's raw footage and selects from among the tapes), naming the bears, trailing them, repeating over and over like a mantra, "I love you, I love you." He gives his bears human traits. He believes they love him too.

One of Herzog's points, which he underlines with his deep authorial male voice-over is that feminized "Timmy" ultimately pays for his romantic indulgences by being eaten by a bear in his final summer. Herzog believes in clear lines. The human world is exact and definable, and for Herzog, so is that of the bears. The bear world is one of instinctual hunger and basic primary needs—food, sex, power. Humans have cultivated and inherited other desires, harder to read, including our need to believe we can cross species boundaries and fall in love. For Herzog there isn't any "secret world" of the bears. Herzog thinks he can read what's behind their eyes and he says it isn't mystical. Their stares speak only of an interest in food.

It is here I disagree with Herzog. Human intelligence and imagination are complex but not exceptional. Wildlife science is beginning to show us that animal worlds are as complex and mysterious as the world of humans. Animal lives are full, with no need for our interpretation, and they may even be open to our empathy. They may understand it and why we reach out to them. The urge to fully merge is always dangerous and maybe ultimately ill fated, but the desire to know and understand animal lives is possibly the only drive toward survival all species share.

Herzog is an admirer of *The Peregrine*. He has written about the book and spoken of its greatness on several occasions. He has praised how Baker never sentimentalizes the birds. I am a little like Baker and Timothy Treadwell. I too want to cross over. My interest in the red-shouldered hawks and the neighborhood they participate in is intense. Is it as intense as Baker and Treadwell? I don't believe so. Not yet, at least. My boundaries are flexible but still intact, though I possess the instruments to break down spatial distances and pop the tops off imaginary boxes, I have yet to break away. I've got a good life here in the human world, settled into the suburb, fully vested, a front row seat for plenty of drama. I am more like Herzog, an observer of those who push to the limits, a creator of a mediated middle space short of sheer immersion. When I talk with my students about Treadwell and the bears, I ask them to consider their own relationship with the wild world. Do they believe in a secret world of bears or hawks? Is Herzog right? Is what we see what we get?

12 February. I pass a sign at a church on the way out of the subdivision: "Know where your treasure is hidden and you will know your heart." A mile later a black Muscovy duck is in the road nodding its head at a flock of smaller ducks in the yard. I see what's coming. It's a busy road. An oncoming car hits the duck and feathers fly. The mangled duck exits from under the car, neck twisting like a live electric wire, rolling, then thrashing into the ditch.

And that guy in the car? He never slows down. I slow almost to a halt. It's like someone's pulled out my power cord, and I blow my horn in warning, scare the flock of ducks back from the road.

I feel it in my chest. I hate that man. Yes, I cry over a dead duck. That death crumples me. My treasure is crushed in the wildly jerking body of that duck hit by the speeding car. My heart seizes like a fist and rolls on to the road's shoulder with the duck. The blame goes back thousands of years. It's the Romans and their damn roads. That's where the real crime started. I hate cars and drivers. I hate speed. He didn't even slow down. He had a chance to. Is it out of proportion to grieve for a duck?

I blame the duck too, whose birdbrain was torqued on hormones leading him into the roadway. But why not blame whatever human long ago domesticated Muscovy ducks? Was it the Aztecs? Why not blame sex, a singular strategy for survival that never mixes well with speeding cars? Or blame winter, the way it collides with spring, exfoliating desire. *Fucking duck. Why do I feel so deeply for you?*

When I was a boy I had pet ducks. My mother bought me a new baby duck every Easter. Not Muscovy, but Pekin, the white domestic kind, all named Hannibal because that's what Daniel Boone's son Israel named his duck in the Fess Parker TV show I watched every Thursday night. Usually two or three Hannibals would be waddling around the yard.

But I wasn't Daniel Boone's son, and my ducks didn't live on a Boonesborough farmstead. My ducks roamed our yard, feral, with little purpose, shitting in the grass, harassed by stray dogs. They swam in an old washtub.

But I learned to love those ducks. They imprinted on me as ducklings and followed me around the yard. They gave me relief from the trauma inside the house. They pulled me out into the yard, and beyond, into the woods. Sometime, following the hawks in the neighborhood, I worry that by psychic extension these birds occupy a similar niche for me as the ducks did. That dead duck never knew what hit it.

14 February. It's Valentine's Day and I love the hawks. There, I've said it. Let the cries of anthropomorphism begin. Yes, I practice and act on an unashamed cross-species love.

16 February. I am several hundred miles north of home at a writing conference. Walking in the city today I looked for hawks everywhere but I saw only geese grazing the mall, sparrows tending the sidewalks next to food trucks, and starlings patrolling the squares of dead winter grass. I looked to the ledges of buildings in hopes of seeing a city peregrine. Only pigeons. I miss the daily possibility of hearing "our" birds every morning back home in the suburbs. Here I wake instead to the warning horn of a backhoe and the wail of an ambulance in the distance. We have built a vast urban world in which we have to work harder than in the suburbs to find nature, but nature's everywhere—the soil turned up by construction, an ancient dark oak sequestered in a fenced square, grass widening the sidewalk cracks, the sky always spreading above, sometimes blue and sometimes cloudy. There is plenty of wildlife here too: a cockroach in the hotel room this morning crawling out from under the bed, and two friends with the flu and another with food poisoning, punching their tickets for a safari in the Serengeti of pathological microbes.

A friend is publishing a book on vultures, and I told her about the two hundred that have been roosting in our neighborhood since Christmas. "Oh," she said, "It might not be the same group every time." She says the flocks of the birds migrate down the flyways in fall and winter and back in spring. "They roost where it's sheltered and the winds are right." Maybe that explains why the size of the group varies, and why some weeks there are days when there are no vultures at all.

She had a copy of her book with her and opened it to the photo section—"Look at this guy," she said. "He's equipped with a solar-powered tracker and we know he flies right over your town several times a year. He could be one of the birds you see."

17 February. Home again, driving past the beaver ponds, among the chilly drainage ditches, a single chorus frog sings, but no others answer. In the distance, to the northeast, as if on cue, the two red-shouldered hawks travel, one calling after the other. Are they still copulating daily as they were before I left? Will I see them at it again?

Then first full rush of light pours out of the east and saturates the bare trees on the ridgeline as I hold my binoculars up and scan the wetlands—in the west mustard yellow transitions to warm gold.

Walking back I take the cut-through road and find the female hawk silent and attentive, perched above the chicken coop again on the same oak, habituated to the neighborhood possibilities (i.e., chicken dinner). In another oak in the front yard the smaller male watches too.

Red-shouldered hawks aren't usually included in the family of "chicken hawks." Usually that term refers to more common bird eaters like the sharp-shinned hawk or Cooper's hawk or often (stouter) red-tailed hawk. Once the buffet opens maybe they will show up too.

Chicken hawks or not, I don't like the developing situation, but how else could it possibly play out? There are many scenarios. Would this neighbor shoot at one of them? If I hear gunshot and find a dead bird would I turn him in? It's not illegal to discharge a gun in the suburb. Surely he wouldn't fire at a hawk when there are neighbors in every direction.

I keep thinking about the other neighbor years ago who made the joke about killing the hawk. Maybe I should tell this new neighbor I've seen the hawks watching his chickens with great interest and remind him of the ten-thousand-dollar fine for harming a hawk. The neighbor keeps the chickens in a coop at night but they free range during the day. There are several scrawny birds that will be easy targets. I don't like where this plot is heading.

By the time I get home the whole lowland is flooded with light, and the sun is inching above the trees. I try to resummon the ease I had earlier about the hawks and leave my worrying behind.

18 February. The year continues to round out. Fifty-five days since winter solstice and thirty-five days until spring equinox. For two days I've walked down to the beaver ponds at sunrise, trying to create some sort of routine or ritual against which to mark the activity of the hawks and vultures. This morning the air was a little cooler, and the vultures at the transmission tower were not so active, huddled together against the chill. Then this morning, just after dawn, between here and the beaver ponds, I spotted the smaller hawk with a rodent in its beak flying north, then landing on an oak to eat it. I'd just walked down to the ponds and back and spotted the bird on my return. As usual, the smaller bird seemed edgy and hopped from perch to perch when he became aware I was watching. He called once or twice, weak whistles, unlike the heated vocals of copulation a few weeks earlier. After the hawk finally settled on a perch, it took about two minutes for him to devour the early snack. No wonder these birds sit and stare down at the chickens. How many mice would it take to equal one chicken? Baker said the peregrines always seemed to be eating. Though he kept track of the bird kills, he had no way to note the number of mice, worms, and insects the birds also ate. With the peregrines there were the carcasses of the bird kills, left littered about, the tasty breast filets eaten away. I'm sure our birds are always eating as well—though this is only the fourth time in fourteen years I've seen them with prey.

20 February. —*I hear you at full dawn nearby. I go outside and look up. The morning light targets your cinnamon breast overhead in a poplar tree in the front yard. My first thought is, "The courting is over and you're finally on the nest." I hope you've settled in nearby as you have done years before.*

21 February. Midmorning and it's overcast but the heat continues to rise. The small birds are returning to the bottoms. From the screened porch I hear an undercurrent of twitters in the nearby brush. The feeder's crowded with titmice feeding. I walk outside onto the deck and I hear a hawk over the floodplain to the southwest of the house. I raise my binoculars and look at the edge of the swamp-forest, scanning left and right through the trees, hoping for a glimpse of the calling hawk. Instead I see only five crows, including one very large one with a ragged right wing. The crow's so large at first I mistake it for the hawk. It's flying with something black in its beak and twice lands in full view to eat, but each time I put my binoculars to my eyes to get a look it flies just out of sight again. By the time I've walked out of the woods and onto the road west of the house I'm in the midst of fussing blue jays massing in a red maple. Two blue birds flit back and forth across the road. Then I hear the hawk again, this time advancing along the creek. I never see it, though I continue to walk in the direction of the sound. Then the female flies in and perches in a poplar between our deck and the river, escorted by five cawing crows.

22 February. A thin shadowy call, probably outside the home range. Then, as if stirred up, the big female screams in from the west and lands on a limb near yesterday's perch, goes quiet, and sits listening for five minutes. The shadowy distant bird calls again, and she seems a little rattled. Then she calls too; the tenor of her cry is broken—wiry but forceful. I retrieve my binoculars but when I return and look up, she's gone. Far off I can hear the other hawk, but no returning cry.

—You've stayed closer to the house the last few days. As I was coming home from work just now you flew from a low perch at the subdivision entrance right in front of the truck, flaring your wings in a daredevil delta glide to pass just feet from my windshield. You landed only twenty feet into the swamp-forest with your back to me and turned and watched as I slowed the truck to a halt to observe. The backdrop against which you perched included a mist of red maple blooms competing with the dark angles of the persistent winter trees.

25 February. Midday, home for lunch, and I take a walk to the beaver ponds. Green is emerging all around me, well beyond February's expectations. Anyone can see spring has arrived quite early. The U.S. National Phenology Network confirms the prognosis with a cloud of creamy dark red covering the map of the southeast; the red means spring will be at least twenty days early. I see that posted on Facebook by a friend. There's a ragged line pushed all the way into West Virginia, Maryland, and Delaware. According to the map in my area, the upper Carolina piedmont, the trees have leafed out three weeks ahead of schedule. South of the house, near the creek, I hear a chorus of trilling American toads. Blue flag irises have already emerged in the swamp-forest.

When I arrive at the beaver ponds there are sixty-seven black vultures on the transmission tower and distributed through the trees. The turkey vultures have migrated north or have roosted elsewhere. It's only the sluggish black vultures that still hang around. As I stand looking at the ponds a red-shouldered hawk cries further to the west. I've moved out of the envelope of trilling toads, but in the wetlands around me I pick out chorus frogs, peepers, and several bullfrogs.

The walk to the ponds has become a needed daily ritual. I explore a little more each time, though the multiflora rose is now leafing out and catches at my bare legs as I wade through the new growth down to the inundated floodplain. As I descend I see that what I've always thought of as a natural dike is actually construction debris dumped next to the paved road—bricks and broken concrete, covered over by decades of soil. Sometimes it feels like if you scratch the surface every accessible roadside acre of the piedmont is a dump. Two hundred years of habitation takes its toll. The water, a few inches deep, has a swirling, purple, oily sheen, but all along the warming edge minnows squirm. Wire grass spikes the shoreline. The black trunks of drowned dead trees score the distance.

I pick my way back up from the water's edge and, on my way home, spot the neighbor with the chickens out patrolling his backyard fence, trailed by two dogs. I approach him and ask about the hawks. When I get closer and I realize it's not the neighbor but his young son, I introduce myself as "the neighbor up the hill."

"I've been watching the hawks for almost a year," I say, and point to my binoculars. "Have you had any trouble with them?"

"We've seen them but so far they haven't done anything," he says as two of the smaller white hens run around his feet and look for holes in the fence.

"I wouldn't worry. I think the red-shouldered hawks are too small to carry off a big chicken, but I'd watch out for a red-tail."

"Cool," he says, and he and the dogs run to the back door.

28 February. I have an insight: I don't have to make this all happen in one year. Baker took ten years. Maybe if enough doesn't happen in this first year of observation, I can keep going and hope that, over a span of years watching these hawks, I will get to know them better and a more dramatic story will emerge. Why am I so intent on something happening? Why isn't it simply enough to observe wild birds for a year? Why does something have to happen? Do there have to be plot points in every avian drama? I've stayed interested in two birds making a living. Is it a story if there isn't tension? Don't they have to nest? Isn't that the only possible step after the copulation of the last few weeks? By deciding to write what happens in a year and not condense ten years into one, as J. A. Baker did, I've made my choice. This local drama must come out of the dailiness. This story must track with my life. But I'm resisting. My hunch is that, now three seasons in, I need to suspend my silly parameters and just let what happens unfold.

Then I hear the hawk crying several times in the front yard and I'm back in the eternal present. I smell the early blooming jessamine and I see their yellow trumpets littering the drive. I wander up the driveway with my binoculars hoping to see the bird that's just called and I run into one of my neighbors walking up the hill. He's been out for a run. I tell him before he asks what I'm doing. "I'm just watching the hawks," I say.

"The crows have been giving them hell the last few days," he answers. "But right there's your bird." He points to the vacant lot northwest of our drive, and he's right. Sitting on a perfect perch, a branch of sourwood parallel to the ground, is the big female, facing south, looking contented and wiping her beak on the branch as if she's just eaten. I watch her for a couple of minutes through my binoculars and she wipes her beak several more times and glances our way. "The past twenty years they've always been here," my neighbor says. "Or at least ones like these."

2 March. This morning the sky is blue and cold, but in our backyard a large straight oak has snapped off twenty feet up in a gust of wind, depositing a pile of limbs in the trail. It will take an hour of chainsaw work to clear a path. I've heard one of the red-shouldered hawks already today, at dawn, in the trees in front of the house, crying a time or two. They must be close by, finding more prey on the warming hillsides. I'm not so nervous about what will happen next. The hawks will nest this year, or they won't. I'll find them or not. This story is whatever happens.

5 March. On the high ridge road, a mile above our house, two red-tailed hawks play tag with the sun. And once they get low enough, the crows join in, dive-bombing from above for their own joy. One hawk spirals up into the blue and then drops, delta winged, close enough to kiss. Then both hawks circle in leisurely loops above. I sit on the tailgate of the pickup in the church parking lot and admire their courting. The congregation's message sign announces, "If joy is a habit, love is a reflex."

7 March. There are only twenty vultures roosting on the transmission tower this morning, the smallest group in two months. Yesterday morning during the misty rain the birds were scattered through the trees and as I drove by they looked like black cocoons hanging there. Today the front's moved through and they're cruising the ridgeline, riding the windy thermals.

I drive by to inventory the vultures, but also in hopes I will stumble into a hawk sighting. Yesterday at lunch a single red-tailed hawk cried once on a cruise past our house. Was it one of the two I'd seen courting on the ridgetop several days ago? It's been three weeks since I saw the two red-shouldered hawks copulating. I'm still nervous that they're on a nest and I won't find them. One hawk study suggests that in the eastern United States egg laying commences in late March, with incubation lasting about thirty-three days. Based on these numbers, I have some wiggle room. A square mile isn't a huge area, and I should be able to find the nest in that space.

I hear one of the bird's noisy announcements and triangulate on it by driving up and down the grid of streets in the subdivision. I call Drew and put him on speakerphone so he can hear the cries. "That bird's stirred up," he says. "It's like it's being challenged or something."

"I'm circling the block, following the sound," I say.

"If you drive around one more time, somebody's going to try and sell you something," Drew jokes.

I finally locate the bird sitting in a big oak. For five minutes it screams, then it takes off and flies further north.

"So maybe it's not one of my birds," I say.

"You keep calling them *your* birds," Drew answers. "You know you're profiling. You don't know if that's your bird or not."

8 March. Baker suspended his life to spend ten years watching peregrines in Essex. I like the honesty of my one year's reporting, one journal laying out the day to day, more than Baker's picking and choosing from among over three thousand days. His approach seems more like fiction, like shaping a novel. My one year feels like a high-wire act. If I somehow miss the birds nesting it will be as if the reader is watching a play and the main character walks out of the script and doesn't come back for the whole last act. Baker would probably chuckle at my lack of patience. What are ten years of a life to produce a book that's today considered a masterpiece?

As if to mock me, I hear the faint cry of a red-shouldered far off to the south, somewhere out over the floodplain. Is it a bird going between hunting and the nest? Is it a bird moving along the edge of one or more territories? What is there to learn of patience from watching birds? I learn about the world by paying attention.

9 March. A brassy, cold morning. The sky is gunmetal blue. At seven-thirty a.m. I hear the red-shouldered hawk crying and then a scattering of crows begins to assemble too. They caw from different corners of the floodplain. When I walk onto the back deck I see the crows, five of them, beelining due north. The sun flares to the east through trees still bare with winter. The crows have set disturbed transects in the chilly air and gang up in nearby trees. The hawk calls again. I swivel my head and triangulate on the sound and realize it's in the front yard. I walk through the house and onto the front porch. One more call helps me catch a glimpse of the solitary hawk leaving a tree near the one I had hoped would become their nest site, just northwest of the house. The crows follow, bullies throwing their insults back and forth.

6:00 p.m. The bookend of the day. A band of silver evening light left along the river, treetops dark above it, and below, gradations of green and brown trunks spotted with the last sinking patches of sun. Against this backdrop the red-shouldered hawk cries three times, first upstream, then, after I see it, it flies like a needle puncturing the light, downstream, parallel to the porch, where it lands and sits silently above the river until what silver the fading evening spins among the late winter limbs dissolves into the dull brown corduroy.

10 March. As I drive out at lunchtime I have the windows down and the radio off, a precaution I always take against indifference to the land. Because I am prepared, I hear crows and follow their alarm upward to see a hawk with a silver-gray breast preening in a tree. I slow the truck and pull over. The hawk is in the oak grove on the slope across the road from the beaver ponds. The two crows dive-bomb the unexpected visitor. With the crows' caws I anticipate the tangerine breast of a red-shouldered hawk but instead see a bright white-breasted bird perched in the faraway tree. A large Cooper's hawk, maybe even a goshawk?

The bird sits patiently with a good view of the wetlands as the crows tag-team it from above. Its presence is a novel surprise. Our hawks' home range is a space other species of hawks pass through. Competing creatures press in from the margins or drop in from above. This year I've seen three or four different types of hawks, plus the owls, of course. Once I've zeroed in on the bird it stares down at me. Through the binoculars the oak limbs form a halo and make it difficult for the crows to get a good angle of attack. It's very windy, and I'm sure that makes for even more difficult aerodynamics if you're a crow.

The habits of Cooper's hawks and goshawks are more mysterious to me than those of red-shouldered hawks. I text Drew, who tolerates my ignorance, but he doesn't answer back this time. He leaves me to my own speculations and observations. I open iBird Pro and type in goshawk, then Cooper's hawk. I read the thumbnail text and look at the pictures, though the real bird in the real tree is far away and too obscured for research. I drive the truck down the road a little farther and get another view and more details. Of the goshawk the field guide says "bigger, fiercer, wilder than a Cooper's hawk, with short, broad wings"; it also has the ability to move with agility when hunting. The text compares the size of the Cooper's hawk to a crow, but this bird is bigger than its tormenters. Goshawk? All I can really see is the light breast bright in the sun and the black hammer of the crow dropping over and over from above. When I look down to get my camera I miss the mystery hawk leaving the perch. I spoil the opportunity to observe some more. Later, Drew texts a comment on my grainy picture. "Big female Coop," he reports.

11 March. Last night the temperatures plunged to freezing and there's barely a patch of pink in the dawn sky, but already the crows and the red-shouldered hawk are at each other in the front yard.

14 March. Driving home from school I pause at the stoplight at the intersection a few miles from our house. The red traffic signal holds a long time and to my left a few dozen slate gray pigeons drop from a wire to the mulch around a water oak. As the lane of cars next to me turns I think about an article I read by British nature writer Mark Cocker in which he describes peregrines hunting in an English marsh. His "wild bird blood" and his widgeons, dunlins, and ruff "boiling up" in the faraway marshes return to me to the complex intersection with its fleet of commuters and its suburban flock of foraging rock doves.

Then, just when the light changes, the pigeons flush, like something has thrown a switch on the whole assembly. What has triggered their "panic," to use Cocker's word—is it simply the sudden movement of the mundane traffic? Then, cutting low across my windshield, a sharp-shinned hawk, in swept-wing glide, adjusts slightly with the breeze, calm and lethal, and heads straight for where the pigeons scatter.

16 March. A red-shouldered hawk was active around the house the last few days. On Saturday I saw the big female sitting on a dogwood branch up in the neighborhood northwest of here; then the next day I saw her sitting on the ground in my neighbor's yard, and the following night, near evening, I hear the bird crying, down by the river. I hope there's going to be some sign they're nesting, but so far, no luck.

When I was in college I had an English professor who joked that art is mostly about two things—birth and death. He said that somewhere in the crannies and creases of every great poem, painting, novel, sculpture, or song, you could locate this theme-of-themes, this eternal dance between the beginning and the end of the human earthly existence. You're either busy being born or busy dying. That's how Bob Dylan put it.

A few years ago I was sitting in my third-floor office at the college where I teach. I was lucky to have a corner office and two windows. Just before lunch our resident red-tailed hawk landed ten feet from my east window and sat for fifteen minutes before a gray squirrel (even closer to my window) made a fatal mistake: it left the safety of the nest to head down the oak.

The patient hawk swooped down and nailed the gray squirrel from the higher branch a few feet away, but then the hawk skidded past the branch and fell until it wedged itself in the enclosing branches of the oak with its wings extended, only a few feet from my window. The hawk was hanging there by its wings with its talons wrapped securely around the squirrel's head, and the rest of rodent was bobbing helplessly below. The bird looked over at me several times, reached down and pecked at the squirming squirrel, and continued to hang there. Each time the hawk pecked at the squirrel the body of the big bird slipped a little lower among the limbs that were holding it. Would it fall, spiraling down another forty feet to the ground? Would the squirrel finally die and stop its disorienting squirm?

I watched in fascination as this little death drama unfolded outside my office window. It was late winter. A squirrel was busy dying, while the hawk was busy with life. After hanging there for about ten minutes, the branches finally gave and the hawk broke free and plummeted toward the ground, still holding the squirming squirrel, but the great hawk wings caught air right before it hit the ground and it flew off to finish its lunch under a big cedar tree.

17 March. For three days now the wind has picked up, and the temperatures have dropped below twenty-five each night. The water in the birdbath is frozen solid in the garden, though only three weeks ago the weathermen were proclaiming early spring. Brutal cold for tender leaves. All the blueberry blossoms have wilted in the side yard, and the rhododendron's leathery leaves have pulled in tight like they often do in January. Is it too easy to simply blame climate change? I know it's important to maintain distinctions between climate and weather. Weather in March and April in the upper piedmont has always been fickle. In my sixty years I remember many cold Marches. That's mostly what destroyed the peach industry in our area. Late frosts killed crops year after year before most farmers gave up and grew housing developments in their fields.

One April, about a decade ago, we had a freeze at Easter with temperatures in the low twenties that burned the emerged young leaves of all the hardwoods. It was almost mid-May before a new set of replacement leaves pushed out. That was an odd spring. Drought followed that summer, and the trees, stressed by the late freeze and the lack of water, struggled, and many died.

As I walked the dog, a sharp-shinned hawk tilted back and forth above us in the wind until I lost it in the sun. Then the yard was full of robins. Had the hawk followed them in?

18 March. The remaining colony of roosting vultures at the beaver ponds is down to about twenty-five. They seem to prefer lounging in the trees, but a few still perch on the crosspieces on the tower. I check it every day on my way home. During the day the transmission tower and trees are always vacant. The vultures radiate outward looking for food. Any time I see a vulture over town (about five miles west) I wonder if it's one of "ours" from the beaver pond roost.

On the road just before the crossing the river downstream, I chance upon another twenty-five black vultures feasting on the carcass of a dead deer. Cars slow to watch the feast. While ten or twelve gorge on the roadkill, the other dozen or so wait below in the swale. As I pass, one bird drinks from the backed-up water of the beaver ponds, while others stand around, either already full or looking for a chance to hop up and chow down. I'm relieved by the sight of all these vultures disassembling the carcass of a deer I've probably seen in our own backyard. All winter I've worried about whether the vultures have enough to eat, and this assures me, at least for a while, that their bellies will be full.

This river crossing is about a mile below the Beaver Pond roost, and I wonder how one black vulture alerts another to food. In our fifteen years here I've seen a dozen dead deer at this crossing spot. Everyone goes too fast here, and so deer/car collisions aren't uncommon. No one ever alerts animal control to the carcass, so the animals decompose by the side of the road. They're almost always discovered by vultures. Do the birds possess some memory of these spots where speed kills, where food is often available? Besides the unlucky deer, I've seen many dead raccoons and possums by the bridge. One spring I watched an adult gray fox carry off a chicken from a house up the hill then over the next week a litter of three gray fox kits got run over in the road as they played in the traffic next to their den.

Black vultures hunt by sight and so a spiraling kettle of birds over a dead deer could be seen at least a mile away against a backdrop of sky. Maybe that's how they locate and share such a feast. I will go back by today at lunch and see how much progress they've made.

10:00 a.m. I hear a red-shouldered hawk as I leave for work, and the cry pulls me out of the truck before I exit the subdivision. Robins are everywhere. Whole squads flow over the lawns. They forage in the yards, working the mulch patches in the grass, turning decayed bark with their needle beaks. I turn my binoculars in the direction of two robins, and they turn to face me, displaying their tangerine breasts.

A friend of mine once told me that he was so poor when he was in graduate school in the 1950s he shot and ate robins. He said they weren't that different from quail, only more abundant and easier to kill. In Italy they roast songbirds on spits, and in season they can be found at fancy restaurants— whole platters full of plump birds, sausage, and peppers. The French eat orioles, the Egyptians, like us, turtledoves and quail. In Cyprus songbirds are caught in orchards on glue-covered sticks that can be mistaken for perches. In Baker's England, of course, the nursery rhyme tells us it was popular to bake blackbirds in a pie. In many European countries the songbird populations have dwindled, a sad combination of culinary taste, habitat destruction, and agricultural chemicals.

Three days before the end of winter, I leave the robins to their foraging and drive past the beaver ponds and count twenty-five more black vultures lolling in the sunshine, mostly on the ground. I stop the truck and I hear a red-shouldered hawk overhead, reminding me I am not here entirely for vultures and robins.

Spring

20 March. Though the season has changed, there is no
alarm going off in the yard, no warm shining curtain to
fall over the last dregs of winter. The temperature is below
freezing again, and the tops of many shrubs are burned
brown from the cold. Bulbs that emerged early in the freak
February warmth now wither, tiny shrunken soldiers lost
in this climate war. The toad lilies were particularly hard
hit—they collapsed in the side bed into a sloppy swirl of
dull yellow.

It's dawn down at the beaver ponds and a few spring
peepers scattered in the marsh are calling, tugging on each
other's love chains. Before I reach the woods, along the
power right-of-way, a small kettle of rising vultures ride a
thermal, and one red-tailed hawk soars with them. They
keep in a tight circle as they climb. The red wedge of the
hawk's tail catches the early spring sun. Then in the lower
trees, along the cleared right-of-way, not one but two
red-shouldered hawks sound off. I pull the truck off the
road and fish my binoculars from the floorboard. I know the
hawks are perched in the distance, but I can't locate them.
It's the first time since their copulation I've heard more than
one red-shouldered hawk at a time and it awakens my hope
they have nested. Isn't that part of what E. E. Cummings
calls the "syntax of things"—nesting, brooding, hatching,
fledging, the turning of life. I missed a great deal of this. I
never had children of my own. For the hawks, is feeling first?
We know that crows mourn, so do hawks love? These are
not scientific questions, though with the right set of experi-
ments, some conclusions could possibly be drawn.

Researchers in England kept European starlings in two types of enclosures. One was a cage with water and food and rich in branches on which to perch. The other cage was small and barren. Each enclosure had dishes of worms, and the birds had to learn to pluck off the lids. Some worms in dishes with light lids were tasty, and some worms in dishes with dark lids tasted of quinine. The birds in both cages stopped flipping the dark lids. Then the researchers presented the birds in both cages with lids with light gray tops. They found that the birds from the enriched cages were more likely to continue to flip the lids. If the enriched birds were moved to the barren cages they became "pessimistic" and wouldn't flip the gray lids. The conclusion was that the "enriched" starlings were optimistic and "happier" than the impoverished birds. Every morning I flip the lid of the day to see what's inside.

I know I sometimes project human emotions onto the hawks and often imagine how their lives go from month to month. I worry about their welfare and wonder where they sleep at night. When we first moved out here, I read in the paper about a woman who lived on a street nearby who fixed scrambled eggs every morning and left them on her porch to feed a local young red-shouldered hawk. I haven't yet crossed over to hawk feeder. It's still an interesting thought, a pet hawk fed on scrambled chicken eggs in an orderly neighborhood, another way to look at the syntax of things in the human-enriched modern world. There are those who don't notice the hawks, those who study them, those who write about them, and those who feed them. The continuum is robust.

21 March. Midday and it's eighty-six degrees. The sky's clear and blue. In only a few hours the lid pops off winter and spring spills over the land. The privet turns green and bolts in the bottoms. Red maple blooms litter the spindly shadows, burned by last week's cold. I roll the truck windows down and the heat presses in, heavy and thick like glue. Even the wind is sticky.

I swing past the silent beaver ponds and a red-shouldered hawk flies right up in front of the truck and settles on a low limb. I pull over and watch through the binoculars. It's the smaller hawk. He sits on the limb facing into the woods and scans the swampy floor below, then tilts his head and looks at me looking at him. It's a moment J. A. Baker would have made much more out of than I do, one of those creature-to-creature gazes—a moment when the bird seems to accept his "predatory shape." Baker's sense of human predation comes from his historic moment. After all, in the early 1960s it looked as if our use of pesticides had doomed what Baker called "the dynasties of the peregrines." It doesn't feel that way to me. The neighborhood red-shouldered hawks are not a dynasty. They are an extended family, as in *mi familia*, settled over eons into the folds of this landscape. The bird's gaze feels like curiosity to me, like kinship, as if it is asking, "Have you been here long? I must have missed you."

27 March. A red-shouldered hawk cry pulls me from the screened porch at lunchtime. I think of it again as one of "our birds"—but once I walk outside I see that there is an entire cast of unexpected raptors in the vicinity. On the trail I startle a mystery bird, a very big hawk, and it quickly joins a kettle of vultures to soar above. Is it a big red-tail? Something else, unidentified? It sure seems larger than a red-tailed hawk, though every time I try to focus on it, the creature slips behind a fan of branches. Once it is airborne it's too high for me to I.D. Then high overhead, as I hear a red-shouldered hawk cry again, three more hawks move in from farther south, two by two, the birds take a spiraling tumble with what I take to be a female. They cavort high against the brilliant blue sky. I crank my head back and watch for ten minutes as they play tag team with the spring sun directly overhead. A white cloud bank floats by like a chunk of the Cliffs of Dover broken loose. The vultures and the mystery bird cruise even higher, nonchalant.

I'm a little perplexed, so I call Drew. "Aren't they more monogamous than that?" I complain.

At first Drew castigates me for going too far with my anthropomorphism and then he reminds me that I don't know for sure which individual bird I'm seeing. "Birds are always floating through, and there's always competition for mates. Sexuality and birds is a fluid thing."

"But red-shouldered hawks mate for life!" I say, sounding a little prudish.

He laughs. "We say they *generally* mate with a single partner but something else happens all the time."

After hanging up I sit on a log. I hear an American toad and then two Carolina wrens playing sonic badminton— back and forth goes the shuttle of their call. Somewhere farther south the four hawks keep up their calling too, high in the sky. Sometimes the courting female almost whistles, but mostly it's the usual three notes of prolonged longing.

Then three green anoles leap from sapling to sapling. Two males and a female? Two females and a male? Three males? Three females? Drew would remind me that in order to really know and fill out the lines of this love poem I would have to catch them and figure out how to determine the gender of a lizard. It doesn't matter. Somehow we are all here together. "When it comes to bird sex, all bets are off," Drew texts back.

29 March. Blue skies again and warmer temperatures. Another day of noontime courting for the hawks. I hear the female crying frantically south of the house and see her fly low through the treetops in the vacant lot between here and our neighbor's house, and then she banks and begins to climb the thermal. Soon after, performing a dozen circles, she is five hundred feet above the house. I try to watch her with binoculars but it is more comfortable to lie back flat on the deck and shield my eyes to keep watching as she climbs even higher. As I watch, a wedge of geese moves above me. So much action in the sky. The female hawk cries out the whole time, and soon the males appear—two this time—and climb with her. In the sun their wings look pink around the edges. All are crying noisily. I lose her as she and the males drift west over the floodplain. In ten minutes they are back at landscape level, crying as they move about. I miss the tumbling fall together I'd seen the other day, but I am encouraged that our yard seems to be some sort of red-shouldered epicenter. If a thousand-foot maypole ascended from our yard into the sky it would be as if they were circling it. Maybe she will nest here. Her world seems to spin around this place as an axis.

1 April. The female red-shouldered hawk has been entertaining three males all week with fast darting flights between perches, followed by aerial acrobatics and high frivolous cries. Today she is dateless, solo, and circling the perimeter of the yard—her circuits keep with the cardinal directions, beginning in the north, as if she were performing a spell.

The high today will be eighty and there are squads of bumblebees in the yard for the first time. "Bee dirigibles," a friend calls them. There are even a few swallowtail butterflies flitting through the woods, looking for early blossoms. The dogwood blooms are tiny cream torches visible even in the dark before dawn. This is the magic week when every fuse is lit and the light and color seep from within. Nothing tarnished remains of the dull cast of worn-out winter evergreens. The privet in the wetlands has changed the most—the splatter-patches of dull moss and pickle shades have disappeared, replaced with lime, mint, seafoam, and harlequin greens.

Goldfinches returned to the feeder yesterday, and the warmer weather has brought out the snakes too. I saw my first dead one of the season in the neighborhood—a black rat snake crushed flat on the road paralleling the beaver ponds—and I've passed a black racer on the creek trail several times, coiled next to a rock crevice for safety in the lingering stupor of early spring. Spring in the blood moves the animals around and makes them more vulnerable. This warmth will be the last thing many living blobs of protoplasm register. They'll become a meal for one that makes it through to summer.

8 April. The hawks have been distant neighbors for days. I've heard their crying off and on the fringes of the subdivision. They often start to the north and then beeline (or should I say hawkline?) for the south, screaming the whole way. But the week wasn't without its natural drama. Yesterday morning the overnight winds left us a gift across the entrance to the neighborhood, a ninety-year-old fallen red oak, the green leaves brought low, transparent, and the size of cat paws. Some unknown chainsaw artists had cleared a car path by nine a.m. Thanks be to them. I stopped as always to look at the tilted root ball for artifacts, as if it were a little unexpected door opening down into the landscape's past—soil turned up, popped white roots exposed.

All the other big oaks that were cut down to build our house were of a similar age. So the succession from old fields to oak-beech hardwood forest started about a hundred years ago here and left us this forest we live in today. Were these yards cotton fields until 1915 or was it even then a recently cut forest? Settlement here began in the late 1700s, and that leaves a big gap of one hundred and fifty years, almost enough time for two oaks this size to grow up. Our lot borders the bottoms, and I am guessing it would have been heavily farmed in the nineteenth century. Maybe scrutiny of LIDAR images can tell me something more. This time, in the opened-up hole, I find one squared-off quartz stone, the same material as the points I've found around the house. Natural fracture? Evidence of paleo hunters on the land? There's one more horticultural bonus—an uprooted jack-in-the-pulpit that I plant in our yard.

12 April. I have reached an impasse with the hawks. They have gone very quiet, and I am not writing as much, and I imagine (pray) it is because the female is now on a nest, but I have not located the nest, so she has dropped out of the narrative. Poof. This puts a huge crimp in my July-to-July plan. (Such fearful symmetry.) It looks now like I will have to parallel *Peregrine* more than I wanted. I have less patience than Baker. His book condenses ten hawk observation years into one representative "year." I still want my story to have more immediacy, to happen in one "real" year, so it will feel more direct and authentic and naturally historic, and not so constructed. Maybe I can still pull it off. Maybe I will wander into the nesting site by happenstance or triangulation, and the year will be back on track and will roar forth again. If I observe carefully enough, I should be able to figure out which quadrant of the home range the hawks are now hanging out in. Another possible scenario is that this particular female is a failed nester and she has never raised a brood. As a character she is an avian femme fatale, a mysterious sky-seducer, for decades leading males into compromises, dangers, and deep dives that never pay off.

Betsy always kids me about how susceptible I am to the idea of natural symmetry, return, balance. I have an almost fairytale interest in doubles, triples ("three magic beans!"), and this might just be my favorite literary trope. We watched Jim Jarmusch's *Paterson* last night and the director used as visual cues the recurring sighting of twins as well as Paterson's artist wife's recurring paired circles and wavy lines on cloth, curtains, and cupcakes. In the film, pattern alerts us that we are in the land of poetry. And yet I have never liked traditional forms. But I like the idea of form, and what could be more traditional than the rounded year, with birth in the spring? We will see.

13 April. At lunch I hear the hawk crying frantically out beyond the yard. Only the flimsy green screen of spring foliage softens the complaint. This morning I dipped back into *The Peregrine* and saw clearly that these red-shouldered hawks are not at all like Baker's falcons; on his every page it seems their silence is like a weapon cast from above into the troubled flocks below. These red-shouldered hawks don't seem to care if the shrews hear them calling. Maybe there is even some intuition that the snakes and frogs, with their inner ears, can't sort threat from the background noise processed by their rattling skulls. This noisy bird announces its every mood. Its cries pour over the yard like sheetwash from a storm.

But there is something different now. What I hear in the home range are not the plaintive cries documented by me in January, nor the amorous cries and whistles of March, nor the cries without competition among the rafts of February's silent vultures; instead the present cries are a sort of all-out spring desperation. At least that's what I speculate. I know I am probably projecting my own complex and rattled animal interior onto the red-shouldered hawk. Last night I dreamed of wild animals in the yard, an owl and her fledgling in a tree outside the window, a bear and her cub pursued by dogs, even a wounded lion that transformed into a jaguar chased down by two hounds.

After the dream, I thought back to the question Betsy asked me in the fall: "What does it mean when a man's heart yearns so much toward wild animals?" This garbled, frantic dream menagerie is no Disney movie. The unconscious images inside me are of both birth and death, the silent safety of the nest and the mad cacophony of hunting and feasting.

14 April. The biggest crow I have ever seen just landed in the yard. It's not a complete stranger. It's been hanging around for three days. The first time I saw it I was in the bedroom and watched it drop from a low limb to the ground below the bird feeder. It looked as big as an eagle. Then yesterday I was on the deck and it swooped overhead. I thought it was the shadow of a vulture. Then today when I saw it I asked out loud, "Is that a *raven*?" The bird's a loner, which I've never seen with crows here. They're always in a gang. This is one impressive bird.

A glance online shows me that a raven is not out of the question. The common raven was once a regular in our upper piedmont, pushed to "uncommon" status in recent decades by all the things I'd expect: human persecution (farmers often thought they killed infant lambs), logging, and development. They've done well in some areas of the suburban South because of readily available garbage, irrigation water, and abandoned houses, which they use as roosts. Though protected under the Migratory Bird Treaty Act, they receive no federal status. Some of the bird protection groups consider common ravens a "low priority species" in most of the states around us. Did this raven drift in with the visiting vultures? Ravens are known to consort with vultures, relying sometimes on the same shared thermals, following the vultures to their prey. And they're said to nest in areas frequented by peregrine falcons too, so Baker is never far away.

This raven might be a neighbor. There's at least one record of common ravens nesting only about forty miles west of here as recently as 1988. Several sources online claim they still nest there. Back in 1986 the nest was described as bulky and placed deep in a crevice on a crag near the summit of a rocky dome, set amid mature oak forests and hemlocks. Today the hemlocks are probably dead, but the ravens may still be around. Maybe some spring I'll drive up and see if the nest is still there.

I don't know why it excites me so much to think there may be a raven in our yard. It's possibly the disappointment I'm feeling at my not finding a red-shouldered hawk nest, that the birds are carrying on their lives out beyond me, hidden somewhere in this small home territory I felt I had come to know. And then this big black, magical trickster shows up, steals the show, and focuses me on immediate bird life again.

Later. The raven has been hanging around the backyard. Is it auditioning for my hawk journal? I just watched it chase a black racer through the woods with its wings up, a bulky shape slaloming downhill between the slender saplings. At first I thought the racer was chased by a strange, inky black mammal, like a black fox with wings. Then when the shape made the turn and headed downhill toward the fence I saw it was the raven. It was close enough I didn't even have to pull out my binoculars.

The ribbon of snake had the advantage in the steep terrain. Losing the race, the raven shifted from fox to eagle, flew to a low limb, pinned its stare on the streaking snake, and almost beat it to the brush pile with two extended wingbeats. Then the raven strutted around the pile, panting, waiting for the snake to exit, but it never did. Ravens in Native American legends are creatures of metamorphosis, and it's said that they symbolize change and transformation. That's not hard to believe after witnessing this race. Then, as if on cue, in the nearby woods, one of the red-shouldereds called, and the raven flew away.

16 April. Easter Sunday. Driving out to eat lunch we slowed to a halt on the hill in front of our house to watch a dozen black vultures, maybe the last platoon that's left of January's neighborhood army. They took turns finishing off a freshly killed gray squirrel and didn't seem concerned that we were maybe in a hurry. While one pulled and nipped at the rag of pelt, gristle, and flesh, the others either strutted in the street or lounged like roosting chickens in the leaves along the verge. One young grandstander ogled the assembly and waited its turn on an overhead branch. I'd heard the panicked neighbor dog all morning, a nervous, adolescent Boykin, but just figured it had been abandoned by the family for Easter, not knowing that this sanitation squad was at work just outside the electric fence.

The bad judgment of squirrels is often on display on this hill, which is used by neighborhood kids for sledding when it snows. The same teens in cars gun it in all seasons making it the fairway of rodent death. How this narrow passage between two wooded safeties must have shaped our neighborhood population squirrel dynamics we'll never know. That's way beyond the budgets or brains of most citizen science. But one thing is for sure: many squirrel dynasties have been cut short here, flattened on the pavement.

Last year I watched the king of yard squirrels die of old age. For almost a decade he had been the meanest big male in the yard. It was easy to spot him. His tail looked like it was tipped in white paint. He must have survived hundreds of road crossings. Then one day in spring I saw him for the last time. He looked like Lear as he stumbled around the side yard. When I walked close up I could see how old he really was—his pelt was badly groomed, his teeth had grown long, and he was completely white around the whiskers. His eyes looked milky calm.

When I approached, the old man just trundled on through the leaves and didn't try to climb the nearest trunk. He turned his head toward the sound of my footsteps but kept using his nose like a cane to smell his way along. If he had been a human king in that condition he would have been talking to himself. I found him stiff an hour later.

This is the day Christ is said to have risen from the tomb but the only resurrection here is squirrel purée brought back to life as vulture flesh. The winged actors out front are enough to make make holy day believers squeamish. The leads in our passion play have scaly heads, black frocks, and a taste for what's palpable over time.

20 April. Midmorning. Out of town for two stormy days with wind and rain from the southwest. Everything feels green and refreshed. I was greeted by two red-shouldered hawks noisily spiraling right over the house. One bird's airspace is high, about five hundred feet above, and the other circles a couple of hundred feet below. They climbed into formation from the north, and continue to call, drifting in that general direction. If there is a hawk nest, it may be downstream, in the deeper woods below our subdivision. I need to spend some time over the next few weeks wandering the edge of the neighborhood down there.

The birds are very noisy this morning, the most vocal I've heard them in weeks. Is this overheard conversation about sex? About territory? About neither? My ears are not accustomed to such sounds. Is this net of cries symbolic communication or are they simply crying out of irritation or desire?

Later I text to tell Drew about the noisy hawks overhead this week and he writes back, "I do often wonder if other animals might experience the world in profoundly different ways. I guess that's sort of a given to some degree. But it could be pretty extreme. Does the hawk 'see' your house, your deck? Not as house or deck obviously . . . But do they appear as what they are at all?"

22 April. Earth Day. Walking the trail downstream from the house I scare up a hawk. "Is that your bird?" Betsy asks. "No, a marsh hawk," I say as the big dark bird flies away, and I see that white rump patch plainly. Of course, that's the old name I still use out of habit.

We stop for the dog to drink and I see a small northern water snake swimming in the shallows. "A two-snake day," Betsy says, reminding me of a king snake we'd seen nosing through the front flower beds earlier. I tell her that I'd also seen a box turtle on a mission behind the house, high-stepping once it saw me. "It's the spring heat warming up their cold blood."

We walk all the way to the bridge and I notice the cliff swallows are back, but in diminished numbers so far. Last year by late April there were dozens of pairs of birds repairing mud nests under the bridge. Today we only see four.

28 April. The sky is gray, but near the ground the fresh grass in the meadow glows. The thick scent of honeysuckle wafts in from the fence line. Early in the morning I see the first rose-breasted grosbeak of the season. The flame of color is a shock at the feeder. It gorges and gorges on seeds. I hear the baffle rattling and think a squirrel is trying to climb up. At 10:30 the hawk is sitting on the crook of the backyard bird feeder. The grosbeak is gone and cardinals keep their distance. I didn't see the hawk's approach or whether it made an attempt to nab a songbird or not. Good circumstantial evidence though. Maybe the bright red flag of the grosbeak's breast pulled it in from the woods and, as I have hoped, there are chicks to feed.

The minute I come out on the porch, the hawk flies south into the floodplain. I follow the retreat as far as I can until the woods close around the bird like a fist. Then soon after I hear several cries, and it's gone.

2 May. Rain for two days. Winds have whipped in and out as squall lines moved in from the southwest. Everything's sodden. Driving the wet roads to school I scare up a large hawk west of the house. The hawk is on the wet ground, and when I pass, it mounts the air and shoots through the trees, escaping the whispering road. All I see are its dark back end and two thick brown wings mottled with white when it banks and disappears. I text Drew, and he calculates, "On the ground, large, stout wings. An accipiter probably. Too big to be a sharp-shinned. Less likely to be a goshawk. Sounds maybe like a big female Cooper's hawk. You've seen one near there before."

As I drive to school I think about the red-shouldered hawks. I'm scrambling every day to stay connected to their world and I'm happy to get the scrap of an outlying raptor in a cutover creek field to grab my attention. I'm listening and watching at home, the hawk epicenter, but as the green fringe of full new leaves closes in around the house it's getting harder and harder to see them. Spring has a way of obliterating the sightlines of early March. Their calling has diminished as well.

Maybe it's time to do a little analysis. I've heard the birds mostly in the mornings, and they have often been north and northeast of the house. That's what makes me believe that the birds are maybe nesting up there somewhere. Next week, or the next, that will be my task: to walk through those woods again and see if I can find them.

7 May. Blackberry winter. Forty-eight degrees when I set out. The sun bleeds from the east through wet woodlands. I head into the sparkling. I'm scaring up cardinals as I walk on the trail behind the house, and their chatting is all around. There are flashes of red and silver gray through the brush. Is there a cardinal nest nearby? They seem overly excited and anxious for me to move along.

Walking on through shaded meadows on the edge of the floodplain, invasive stiltgrass competes with river cane, pawpaw, and native ripe wild strawberries. Coming down a worn deer trail I hit the little tributary creek and head upstream, and soon begin encountering the little waterfalls, gravely spots giving way to shoals only a dozen feet across. The slope's a little higher there and the invasive plants change from privet to Russian olive, but the pawpaw persists.

Then another hundred yards onward the little creek tumbles over a waterfall, and all around there are mats of jack-in-the-pulpit, many in bloom, the three leaves a bright green. The deer don't browse them, but it's still a surprise to see so many. I clear away catbrier and poison ivy and sit on a perfect stone next to a little seep about thirty yards long, and by the time the muddy seep intersects the stream it's flowing visibly. Is it seasonal or perennial? It's something to check out with periodic visits. The abundance of jack-in-the-pulpit is a sign of moisture. Some of the pulpits are past their bloom, withered and shrunken to dark nubs, but many others are in full glory with parasols of green and purple, striped purple on the inside. My stone seat is both pulpit and pew.

4:00 p.m. I open the screened door and startle one of the hawks sitting on the deck railing, watching the bird feeder. It sits for a moment, considers the intrusion, then flies off with one sharp, coordinated beat of its broad, brown wings spackled with white. The bird launches into the safe distance of the surrounding trees, where it lands on a low perch.

It doesn't fly far though. It stays close enough to keep an eye on me—and on the feeders. Betsy believes the hawks are connected to me somehow, and that they are aware when I'm paying attention and when I'm not. She thinks they come around to check in, to see what I'm up to. There's no way to know the motives of a hawk, but I believe she's right, that I have somehow become accepted as part of their world. I don't think they've ever seen a human being so intent on following their every move. I think that I will find their nest site—if they have nested. And I think that they will accept me watching from a safe distance the raising of their young—if they have young. There is no way to prove this relationship. I know that, and I'm the only one it really matters to. The hawks don't care. Or do they?

12 May. Today, it was misting when I came home at lunch and as I drove up I saw a red-shouldered hawk sitting on our gate, fulfilling the gate's original promise.

Our gate sits at the top of our yard. Some might mistake it for a torii, but we're not Shinto, and so we didn't put it up as a traditional transition between the profane and the sacred so much as a common portal between the cul-de-sac and the mulch path leading to our front door. We had trouble for years with guests walking down the paved driveway, and the gate helped locate visitors in our wide, woody front space. The gate made the mulch more inviting.

This gate is constructed of massive western cedar beams, and has only one crosspiece instead of the usual two found on a traditional torii. It's fastened with red steel plates I had fabricated at a local machine shop and lag bolts I bought at Home Depot. A pileated woodpecker looking for carpenter bees once hammered holes in the beam's face, and I've filled the cavities with flesh-colored concrete, the closest match to cedar I could get.

In Japanese "torii" literally means "bird abode." Since we constructed the gate over a decade ago, it has become a frequent perch for the red-shouldered hawk. And there was a red-shouldered hawk perched atop it today.

As I drove toward the gate, I slowed down and stopped before the hawk saw me. The bird looked sullen. Facing toward the house. Humped against the mist. When it finally saw me, it flew and landed on the corner of the house, near the back door, this time facing toward the approaching truck. I eased the truck into the drive but the bird loosened its wings and with one beat against the damp air bolted around the house. Its wings gyrated as it made the turn. It wrestled with the air as it hugged the corner and disappeared.

I know Baker struggled to define the difference between the savage hawk and the observing human. He watched the peregrines hunting from above, their long trusting falls from great heights, and saw how the other birds scattered. Nothing, Baker remarks, "sustains us when we fall."

For almost a year now I have fallen into these hawks' world. Something about my observing did sustain me. I have caught myself each time before I crashed into them, countered their difference with my own love of the wild. Unlike Baker's peregrines, these neighborhood hawks live right among us. I would not call what they keep "distance." They live at a comfortable remove. I approach as close as possible. If a torii is a portal between the sacred and the profane, is the hawk that sits atop it the sacred itself or its emissary? Is the ceremony it guards one in which I am included? I walk behind the house to see if the hawk is still around but, as usual, there is nothing left of its visit but the rippled wake of its departure in my memory.

19 May. It's been a week. I couldn't wait for the hawks to come to me after this long string of silent days, so I resorted to literary conjuring. It was before ten in the morning, and still cool enough to enjoy a bike ride. Down at the wetlands I slung my binoculars forward and glassed a speck on a tree and saw it was a new species of bird for me—a brown-headed cowbird sitting on the same snag where I'd watched the red-shouldered hawks copulating for the first time two months earlier. It was quiet and I kept listening but the cowbird never called. A grackle flew in and crowded it, but the cowbird hung on its perch overlooking the cattails. I rode on.

As I passed by I was nostalgic for vultures. The last few stragglers had left the electric tower about a month earlier—a few black vultures, maybe young bachelors. Now there was nothing to count. I imagined them all dispersed throughout the Southeast. I wasn't alone in my nostalgia. Every time we crossed paths one of my colleagues who lives close by said, "I miss them."

Then I heard the familiar kyer, kyer, kyer, and looked up and spotted a red-shouldered hawk high up over the neighborhood. I saw there was a tiny black dot in pursuit—blackbird or grackle. I laughed. It was like a war scene from my childhood fascination with World War II, a B-17 being strafed by a Messerschmitt. Even when the hawk picked up speed the small bird put in a burst and caught up somehow. Finally, though, the hawk got some separation, and once it was over the wetlands it dropped like a stone into the far tree line. Is this the nest site? Is it in a tree near the duck pond? It would make sense. There's a food source nearby. I made a note that I needed to float the river and survey that stretch.

I watched for a while, hoping the hawk would reveal itself again, but not a peep. So I rode on up the hill, into the heart of the suburb and then back down into the floodplain. Along the way I scared up a hawk on the roadside and, at first, assumed it was the other red-shouldered out hunting. The bird flew off without any prey. It must have missed a kill. I saw its narrow tail and banded wings and realized it was Cooper's hawk. I wondered if it was the male, the partner of the large female I'd observed earlier in the year. As I observed, the bird banked and accelerated into the green mist of the maturely leafed out lowland forest, staying low, then climbed higher, to disappear against the blur of colluding maples.

20 May. I ventured out again, increasing my neighborhood tour by a mile, adding a rectangle to yesterday's figure eight. Drew calls it "birding by bike." It was later in the day, noonday sun, but like that Englishman Baker I was shadowing, I went out anyway. It paid off. I scared up a red-shouldered hawk as soon as I left the drive. It must have been hidden in a low perch. It was definitely the bike it reacted to. Off it shot at a low angle, crying all the way.

Before I reached the beaver ponds I scared up the Cooper's hawk again—it shot into the comfort of deeper woods with a posse of black birds in pursuit.

The beaver ponds were quiet and hazy, as if summer were hiding in the open cattail marshes. I headed uphill, pushing hard, a good workout, both exercise and natural history. It wasn't until I was twenty minutes into my hot ride, at the end of tracing the route of my rectangle, high along on the ridgeline road, that I began to cruise through a tangled web of birdsong strung from yard to yard—cardinals and mockingbirds were hidden in almost every shrub—and there I also heard a red-shouldered hawk, this time off to the east, in the next suburb over from us; then, as if those calls had lit a fuse, I heard another red-shouldered hawk high above, crying, and, one rung up the sky's ladder, two more birds of prey, too high to I.D.

21 May. Rain kept me inside until after lunch. It's a stormy time. Three days of dark fronts moving in from the southwest. In the bottoms the pawpaw leaves have been flipped up by the wind, leaving their silvery sides exposed. Sodden limbs litter the yard and the drive.

I've always believed that if I watched the foraging flights of the hawks closely enough they would act as arrows pointing me toward the nest. I've never lost hope. I saw the smaller hawk three times today. First, after lunch, when I walked out with the garbage cart to the street, I saw a shadow and looked up to see the one I call the male on a sort of low northwest trajectory headed toward a neighbor's house, with two small songbirds in hot pursuit. The two little birds buzzed around the streaking hawk like menacing yellow jackets. Only when the hawk disappeared into the trees did the birds fall away. Then, an hour later, I took another J. A. Baker bike ride and it paid off. I turned the corner out of the subdivision and spotted the smaller hawk in the wetland, perched on a low limb. Stopping, I noticed it had caught a small snake. It quickly secured the prey and flew due north, generally in the same direction I'd seen it earlier.

So I had two data points, two flight paths. If I could get one more, maybe I could begin to triangulate. I also added this information to a map I'd produced—of the hawk cries I'd heard since the middle of April. I've heard the hawks eighteen times, and they've mostly been north/northeast of the house. And yet these two coordinates had placed them on missions to fly directly back northwest once in possession of prey. Do the hawks have chicks in a nest somewhere in the fringe of woods between our street and the next subdivision street north of us? That was my hypothesis as I tooled around the neighborhood.

Then, after making the loop of the neighborhood on my bike, I headed back down the hill to our street and heard a red-shouldered hawk give a warning call and then retreat in the general direction I thought the nest might be—it wasn't the usual leisurely consonant-heavy keer, keer, keer, or the more frantic kher, kher, kher, but a call much sharper and throatier, as if something were on the line.

26 May. Yesterday I passed a fawn on a trip to town. It was standing in a power right-of-way along the flood plain. As I drove on I watched a Cooper's hawk on an unsuccessful attempt to catch a grackle in some magnolias. On that same trip I stopped and helped a box turtle across the road—a small boost to the genetic pool of that particular reptile. Then on the way back I paused at a traffic light and saw with a side-glance at some rhododendrons the same Cooper's hawk spread flat against the ground, covering some prey. It looked like a hen sitting on an egg, except for the tense wings forcing something down. Near where I'd spotted the fawn I saw a dead doe. The first thing I heard this morning were coyotes in a celebratory chorus. The calls came from the northwest, in the general direction of the wandering fawn.

When reading *The Peregrine* last summer I came across a passage in which Baker seemed to be overly focused on "the darkness of the hawk," as if he believed life itself were not possible without a deep acknowledgement of how it all ends. His narrative described one death after another. The book thrilled me. It deepened my understanding of this essential truth about life and death. When I'd seen the fawn earlier I'd known something was amiss. It was wandering in the right-of-way in midday. Seeing it, I'd fought back a pang of heartache, like a mother seeing a lost child.

We are taught to love each other but to keep our distance from wild animals. We are told not to get too close. To get too close is to lose sight of that line separating the animal world from the human world that Herzog describes. Baker wanted to pass over into the world of the peregrines, but reading his powerful prose I felt that maybe he wanted to join them out of some unnatural desire to leave the human form. I love my wife, but that doesn't deter my heart from crossing the line and following the fawn or the box turtle—or these hawks in my neighborhood.

28 May. It's been three days without either sight or sound of the neighborhood hawks. I worry each time I lose touch like this. I've read the hard statistics, the actuaries that wildlife biologists calculate—a little over 50 percent of chicks survive the first year, and the survival rate declines from there through adulthood as a result of cars, power lines, parasites, and people. That these adults live at all is just short of a miracle. Every day's transaction is a life-and-death negotiation. Praise be to the ones that survive, and praise to the ones that die so that we might love their survival as a species more.

29 May. Today for comfort's sake I imagine a web of red-shouldered hawks, ever widening home ranges, stretching up and down the rivers of the piedmont, endless territories, as far as the tributaries flow. There's something very hopeful about it, even on days like this when I wonder what has happened to the hawks I've been observing.

It's now been almost a week since I've heard the hawks, but there has been no shortage of raptor sightings elsewhere. I went to a friend's house two miles from here to pick up some plants. His property backs up to a feeder creek for the river. Sitting on his patio we talked as usual about deep human things: theology, art, and his avocation, teaching mindfulness. But I wasn't practicing mindfulness or feeling very interested in human things of the mind. I was only half listening, and when I heard a red-shouldered in the distance

I broke in, finally excited. "Hear that?" I said. "That's a red-shouldered. *Your* red-shouldered hawk."

He listened and considered the bird's call, and said, "I've heard that series of notes for forty-three years, ever since we first built the house and moved out here. They nested across the street in a big oak for years."

30 May. Cobalt four a.m. sky. When I step outside to retrieve the morning paper I enter an overpowering tent of gardenia fragrance. The hoots of two barred owls bounce back and forth in the predawn dark, one west, one east.

31 May. Finally, about noon, a red-shouldered hawk cries a few times east of the house. The cry sounds a little unusual—the three notes I am used to, but this time more clipped and nervous. And then about an hour later a squadron of crows goes crazy in the same direction, the whole pandemonium mounting like a riot. So much noise. The trees rattle with it. Through the gaps in the trees I see a crowd gliding in from all directions. It's the red-shouldered hawk causing all this. The crows are mobbing it.

I sit listening for five minutes and then I look up. There are five hawks climbing a thermal over the house. Are these fledglings climbing high on their first thermal? Several of the birds look larger. From time to time the birds whistle one long prolonged note. Then when they wheel between my binoculars and the sun, the broad fans of their tails flare red. Red-tailed hawks. Two crows, stunt pilots, follow them upward, strafing them, dogfighting, or maybe I should say crowfighting.

8 June. A week of cool temperatures and hard rains. There have been several sightings of the hawks and numerous cries from the near woods. I've drawn a crude map showing the hawks circling the yard, the spiral growing tighter and tighter, a data point or two a day, a little sketch, a date, a time, an arrow indicating direction of flight. The hope is that finding that could track the birds back to the long-anticipated nest.

If eggs hatched somewhere, did the hatchlings survive their neonatal vulnerability in the nest? Or did a raccoon or a gray squirrel discover them while the female was away? Did a windstorm topple the nest? Were there two parents tending it?

Red-tailed hawks are known to predate the nests as well—out of hunting impulse and for territory protection. And, of course, there are always owls. I've never seen a great horned in our woods, but there's a pair of barred owls hanging around quite regularly, and I think often about predation when I hear them hoot. I hear the owl just before dawn and I remember the YouTube video of the quiet wings swooping out of the dark, snatching the hatchling out of the hawk's nest.

9 June. Today about noon I hear what is an oddly varied chorus of hawk calls in the same three-cry pattern I've heard before, but these are lower, almost like a cooing back and forth—a sort of call-and-response among a number of birds. I go out in the front yard and follow the sound to the top of the cul-de-sac—and it leads me to two young birds sitting in the big beech tree on the western edge of the pavement. Fledglings! Young red-shouldered hawks! I keep my distance and watch the two fledglings with my binoculars for about five minutes. They have narrow breasts, heavily striped, a washed-out brown-tan, and their heads look almost bald. Finally they glide west, disappearing through the limbs of the oaks on the hillside. Their broad dark wings look out of proportion to the their narrow breasts.

—I'm shocked. You've fooled me all these months. Was your nest in the tree in our yard the whole time? As I approach the fledglings you dive-bomb me from a nearby pine, calling frantically and circling over my approach, your mother genes kicking in.

After the hawks depart I walk down to look at the old nest tree from below. I am giddy. I feel that my story is nearing some sort of dénouement, but I still want proof. I walk a circle around a big oak. There is still a cluttered mass of sticks in one of the upper crotches. On the ground there are no signs they've nested here, no broken eggshells, no hawk void, no feathers. The site of the nest remains a mystery. But the parents have raised two chicks to maturity somewhere very nearby, that's for sure. Could it have been they were active in the nest the whole time and I missed it, right under my nose?

10 June. First thing in the morning I look up a timeline for chicks/fledglings: mating lasts eighteen days or so. The nest refurbishing begins before courtship ends. Then egg laying and incubation for thirty-five to forty days. Both sexes incubate. Then nest departure takes place at about thirty-five days. I go out and look around. I find tiny wisps of hawk feather all over, small downy feathers with a hint of red on the tips blowing through the yard like snow.

I watch from the cul-de-sac. The two juvies are constant residents of the bordering trees, sitting in the low branches. They joust for the occasional snacks from Mama—"feed me, feed me, feed me," they repeat, the salutations baby-like, though their adult bodies are almost fully formed. They are hardwired to hunt, to haul their own talon-caught calories out of the yard. They sweep by on low trajectories; they are like human adolescents unconcerned as to what collisions await. I've read that the young birds fledge and then roost near the nest site for weeks afterward. "Immature birds may wander out of the typical home range."

But I also remember it's likely one of these two young birds won't be alive in a year—the cruel truth of population dynamics. Nature's cost accounting—which of these two narrow-breasted birds will decompose after only a short span? Which one will carry on the age-old fight with the crows, feeding on snakes and amphibians?

6:00 p.m. The juvies hang around all day, crying out. The three hawks cry to the north for ninety minutes. I'm stumped that I didn't know the birds were nesting so near. I'm feeling that maybe I show throw in the towel and admit that I need another year watching these birds and at least blend two years into one, do my own fable making, but no, there's a counterfeeling running through me that says I got exactly what I got, and it's exciting enough to make a story. I have these new living birds now before me.

11 June. 6:45 a.m. The juvies cry in the front yard. They cried all day yesterday and hardly left the beech tree where I first saw them. It's like a nursery out there. I watched the mama bring the two juvies a small rodent she'd caught—and they flew in cooing as they probably would have in the nest each time a parent returned with food. And then, weirdly, Mama ate it. How do they learn to hunt? How do they not starve? Do parents model behavior or is the hunting entirely instinctual? I haven't seen the smaller male hawk around. Do the males take off once the young hawks have fledged? The hawks' noise level was so impressive in the neighborhood yesterday. "The neighbors are probably going crazy," I said. "Probably not," Betsy said. "I'll bet they don't even hear it. Not everybody hears nature's background noise the way you do."

10:00 a.m. The juvies fly all the way around the house, in great crying cacophonies the whole way. One of the young hawks lands on the deck railing, sits there a moment and stares at me. I'm watching, thinking this is a moment of grave danger. Startled, the young bird could fly into our windows. It's happened before and I'm wondering, was that in June? Were those two window strikes (neither one of them fatal) young birds learning the ropes? June is the fledgling month.

10:15 a.m. I walk into woods behind the house and one of the juvies is sitting on the ground, then glides up onto a low limb. I watch, and it watches me. Then it flies to the porch railing, jabbering the whole time. They're flying all around now, getting control of their wings. They're exploring further each hour. I text Drew: "We're in a hawk vortex. How do they learn to hunt?"

"Individualized feeding. Some are crayfish specialists even," he texts back.

I text what I've seen the previous day, "Mama eating the rodent. Go get your own! Do they starve?"

"You'll sometimes see young hawks in bad shape. Survival goes up after first year. They live in rich environments. Lots to choose from. They learn."

"I'm worried about them."

"You're the godfather of this brood."

12 June. 6:50 a.m. Cool and slightly overcast. The juvies have cried for thirty minutes, since before dawn. It's a song of call-and-response, as if in these first few days out of the nest they need to be reassured constantly. The yard's business goes on, even though there are these new neighbors. There are also the usual cardinal songs.

I walk out and watch one of the juvies perched on a low limb at the head of the driveway. It's being tormented by a small songbird. The young hawk looks perplexed and hops from spot to spot on the limb, trying to rid itself of the pest.

It's interesting, and will continue to be, to see them begin to range down into the bottoms. They seem disoriented and dependent right now. How long does Mama feed them? Every day I find more cast-off feathers. They're everywhere that the young birds sit and cry.

5:15 p.m. The only way to describe the constant cries of the juvies is "plaintive." They've been at it close to three days now. Just a few minutes ago I heard one of them kyew, kyew, kyewing from northeast of the house. I just can't stop thinking about how hard it must be to learn to hunt to survive. I say this as our dog Murphy chows down on kibble in the next room.

6:15 p.m. Brittle evening light. No wind. On a walk we see a dead black snake beside the road, blighted by flies. Earlier in the afternoon Betsy had encountered a black snake stretched across the backdoor mat, and I scared it away. The departing snake disappeared into a hole under our steps, which gave Betsy no comfort.

Could this snake on the road be the same snake? It isn't unusual to see roadkill even in our neighborhood, but the posture of this snake is strange. The five-foot snake is frozen in a death strike. The head and one coil of body are pulled back and stiffened in repose. There are milky scales over both eyes as if it had been about to shed. Across the river someone shoots a pistol, target practicing, and I am worried about the juvies. Will they get in the way? I hear them calling just east of us. That plaintive call again, as I've heard all day.

I want to head back, to go inside and abandon the neighborhood to the guns. But I also want to know more about the snake, so I pick it up by the tail and it dances in my hand like a ghost. At first I think I've been fooled and it's alive, but then I realize it's only the tensile strength of the rigor mortis, and its dance is no more alive than that of a recoiling steel spring.

14 June. 6:15 a.m. I am walking on the road out front and I hear sprinklers in a neighbor's yard. Fake rain. The real sky is washed out. I hear one of the juvie hawks once and then everything goes quiet. I sit on the ground and listen. To my left is the dawn, and to my right, the light spreading into the neighborhood. The Carolina wrens fight for attention around me. Three prattle on from the underbrush. Then behind me both the juvie hawks call, separated from each other, one northwest of the house with the sprinklers, the other one further east, behind another neighbor's house. They are calling to each other above the competition of the wrens. This must be close to the nest site up here. Perhaps they still spend the night in the nest yard.

Then the juvie hawk behind the sprinkler house flies east to join its sibling. They are so noisy. Is this their morning greeting? What function does such complaining achieve? Is it hello? Is it I'm here? Now the house with the sprinklers has released its yapping dog. All these sounds blur in my early morning head. I need breakfast. For me it's a bowl of cereal. For the juvie hawks, it's learn to hunt or die.

9:30 a.m. The juvies circle in the bottoms, crying. This morning I saw Mama come in and then the baby talk began.

A feeding. Since 6:45 a.m. they've ranged outward into the floodplain, where I hope Mama is teaching them to hunt.

5:00 p.m. Light rain. The hawks call.

15 June. 10:00 a.m. After a visit to town, I drive up, and both juvies are sitting—one atop one end of the gate, and the other under the crosspiece on the ground. When I approach in the truck they fly, heading south, past the side of the house, negotiating the trees with skill now, but I still worry. Do they get enough to eat? Are they learning what to avoid?

I walk inside but I still hear them and realize they're hanging close by. I go out onto the deck to check on them. There's a call-and-response underway between the two juvies. They respond in turn to my tri-whistles. They take short flights and seem to have questionable judgment about perches. I watch them land and cling to tiny branches. Unlike the adults, who find the best horizontal perches, these young birds perch where they can. Then finally fly off when they perceive I'm observing their clumsy limb hopping. A cardinal and a wren both call. They're saying, Hey, forget the hawks—I'm here!

I think of Baker. He had little of the maternal, of the nurturing, about him. I text Drew: "This project has been my practice. I hear the birds and go find them. I've done this for a year. It's like 'chop wood, carry water.' I don't know what will come of it, but I do it for my love of the discipline."

5:30 p.m. Both juvies are still around. This time there's one sitting on the post on the backyard fence. It's panting a little, drooping. It's ninety degrees, the first time the hawk has ever been this hot in its short life. I am consumed with fretting about them. When will they start exploring more outward? So far they spend most of their time right here. Where was that damn nest?

16 June. 10:15 a.m. The cacophony begins. The two juvie hawks fly so close around the house they really seem to panic. One of them zips along the deck. Now both are in a tree directly in the side yard. A few songbirds fly past, upset that the hawks are here. But they *are* here. They are noisily here. *Where's Mama? Where's breakfast?* The days must feel very long if you're a hawk learning to hunt.

The hawks have a strong pattern of brown on their breast. They just sit and watch. Then they fly northeast—their vocal pattern changing from the long screeching notes to more of a clipped pitch.

Late afternoon. The juvies are expanding their range. I hear them down in the floodplain for the first time—to the south, almost to the river. Raining now.

17 June. 6:30 a.m. The juvies spent the night far southwest of the nest yard. I just heard one calling there—over the floodplain—near the creek. They have ventured out. It must have been exciting. There was quite a storm overnight. Their first one. The leaves on the pawpaw are all turned over, exposing the silvery side. Everything is wet and cool after the heat of the last few days. Will the juvies come back up here this morning, or stay down near the river? It sounds as if they are a couple hundred yards away. I will have to keep listening for the sharp, repeating, gaspy calls as they ascend from below.

12:30 p.m. Leaving for lunch. One of the juvies is sitting on the fence railing outside the back door. It flies to the black gum tree and sits, its wings extended upward, and I'm watching it play hide-and-seek with a gray squirrel on the other side of the trunk. It nearly pounces—its yellow eyes on high alert. I guess I don't have to worry any more about whether they have the hunting instinct. It's also paying close attention to several large white moths flying past as well, as if it sees those as a food source, and to another gray squirrel on the ground nearby.

Finally it sees me watching. There is a powerful fierceness in its eyes as it looks straight at me. It picks up its wings and peeks around the trunk, and the squirrel scoots the other way. It reminds me of squirrel hunting in the piedmont woods, how you toss a stick on one side of the trunk to get the squirrel to circle into your sight.

18 June. 6:15 a.m. One of the juvies cries early, to the northwest of the house, back near the beech where I'd first seen the young hawks days before. Last night I heard both of them to the southwest around sundown. I haven't seen the parents in a week, not since I saw Mama feeding the newly fledged birds. Two days from now we'll be heading to Detroit for five days. Maybe in Detroit I can finally commune with some city hawks.

9:00 a.m. Sometimes it's as if the two juvies are in a verbal ping-pong match. Their calls bounce around in the side yard. Sometimes the calls are frantically sharp, and other times they slow way down. Every once in a while the crows kick in. The hawks' presence causes agitation in the crows. I can make nothing else of it.

Lunch. One of the two juvies is up the hill to the north near the ridgetop—sitting on the ground. These young birds like to sit on the ground.

4:00 p.m. Betsy and I walk into the front yard and both hawks are sitting in low perches to the west. The one perched on a sourwood lets us get very close and observe. It's the one with the most distinct breast pattern. I'm taken once again by how narrow their breasts are and how broad their wings.

19 June. 4:30 p.m. Warm and muggy. The yard is quiet when I come out. I haven't seen the birds all day. Then after I walk the dog one of the juvies leaves a perch in the lot east of the house and shoots rocket-style through the trees, startled or agitated by my passing. A path through the trees. An escape. The actual air holding up so much—the full experience of being bird.

Today a friend wrote, "I've been wondering about you and the birds. Am thrilled to hear the young birds sitting around your house looking at you looking out. Hey, who is studying who? What kind of scribbling does their journal contain? 'The crazy man is back . . .'"

20 June. 6:45 a.m. I walk outside. First I go to the front yard. One of the juvies is calling frantically, over and over. I spot where it's perched—a large poplar at the lot's front. Then down behind the house the other juvie lets loose an answer. Back and forth they call, the sound ricocheting like an echo. As I turn to look for the other hawk, the bird leaves its perch and flies overhead. I look up and see it, remember how Baker describes the peregrines as crossbows, but I think of these birds more as crucifixes, a symbol of faith and an aid to prayer.

I pause and chase the other bird for a moment. It hops in short flights from poplar to poplar, from one perch to another, halfway up the canopy, calling often. When the quiet descends I can hear the distant call of a third red-shouldered, off to the east.

8:30 a.m. When I drive into the subdivision from the kennel where Murphy will stay during our trip to Detroit, a juvie is sitting on the top of the lamppost at the entrance to the subdivision. When I pass, it wings south.

Summer

23 June. Detroit. I watch peregrines hunting from the old GMC tower. The first morning a fellow conference-goer staying at the hotel mentioned he'd seen a peregrine on a ledge at the top of the GMC building. The second morning it was raining and I sat in our room with my pocket scope and spotted the perched bird. I sat and watched for an hour and sketched in my journal, hoped to see one of Baker's brilliant stoops, but all I saw was a wet urban falcon huddled against the rain on a high concrete ledge, a resting bird. Then a second falcon flew in and the first bird perked up, as if they were a tag team, and dropped off the ledge, disappearing around the building's corner.

On this, the third day, the same conference-goer said he'd seen the falcons again—two adults and two juveniles on the front of the building. I look for them, but never spot them. I remember how when Baker wrote in the 1960s he fully expected the collapse of the falcon populations. I realize that my year has at least been punctuated with a spirit of grand hope. My ecosystem isn't full of zombies. My hawks are living birds.

25 June. 3:00 p.m. Upon our return home the birds are all around. I hear them to the east at first, but Betsy thinks it's not the young one calling. She says the three notes are clearer and more direct. They are not the frantic cry we heard before we left.

Then we hear a bird that sounds more like how we remember the juvies sounding—and then two birds are into a call-and-response—"I'm here. I'm here. I'm here."

We walk the dog to take the temperature of the neighborhood since we departed and find a young crow dead in the street. It's on the edge of the road, so likely a car strike—the teenagers have nearly hit me on this hill, so why not a young crow? The crow's head looks relaxed into death—but there's a yellow-bodied fly on its black eye even though the open eye still has a bright sheen.

And then I conjure up the hawks. We hear one hawk, then the other, and continue our circumambulation of the neighborhood, triangulating on the two birds all the way. I am in my head mostly, though, thinking about the crow. I try to pry myself free of introspection but I can't. I carry on a strange poetic dialogue with the hawks inside my head:

I can track you if you will speak.
You are mistaken. I have no voice. I am another kind of kingdom.
I know my Darwin. We are kin.
I am young. I may not live another month. There are statistics. Data gathered.
I watch your every move.
You believe in the future. I grasp this moment.
The woods are too dense to see you.
Space is infinite. I know where to enter.
Have I wasted a year?
Your territory expands and contracts like mine.

26 June. Before noon one of the hawks rests on the gate. Little calling today. Tomorrow the heat is supposed to rise.

27 June. 9:30 a.m. I have walked to the second cul-de-sac. I sample the sticky air, wander a little off course into the woods at the far undeveloped end, and something jumps— several somethings—hopping out of the olive bushes. It's several gray squirrels foraging unexpectedly in the shade. I examine the olive branches and they're weighted heavily with ripe berries. This might explain why there are so few gray squirrels under the bird feeder—there's bounty in the deeper woods. I try one of the purple berries—very sweet and juicy with one good-sized pit. I'm surprised. I've never noticed them before—this is an important fruit source for wildlife as we head into the dog days of summer. I'd imagine the deer eat them—as do many birds, possums, raccoons, and coyotes. Pondering the berries makes me rethink, on the spot, in situ, the idea of "invasive." These widespread nonnatives are offering a food source fully integrated into the landscape. Should we break that chain by eradicating it?

I walk back home and Google this plant. I check three or four sites, in what passes now for research. And what of this lowly Osmanthus, this upstart, out-of-place olive bush with its many virtues? It's long lived. Virtually pest-free, with one native cousin: what's called "the devil wood," *Osmanthus americanus*. False holly. Sweet holly. Sweet olive. Osmanthus goes by many names. It is a fine choice for hedges, hence its popularity in the old days, when hedges were more popular. A native not to our piedmont hillsides but to China, Japan, the Himalayas, it can live thirty to fifty years and has been cultivated in Asia for twenty-five hundred years. The plant collector André Michaux brought it to South Carolina in the late eighteenth century, along with other more favorable garden and yard ornamentals—crape myrtle, camellia, mimosa, and gingko. I went out looking for hawks and instead found the deep history of a plant.

28 June. 8:30 a.m. Tomorrow is the last day of my hawk watching. An entire year has passed. I just saw one of the juvies in the front yard. It cried loud and flew north into the flood plain.

29 June. 7:00 a.m. In the suburbs it's possible to listen for the wild. We live on the side of a bowl and the sound bounces all around. The birds compete with the human noise. The soundscape is a cloth woven of more than one strand—if I get up early enough I hear the two neighborhood barred owls calling each to each, north to south. An hour later I hear the construction horn on the heavy equipment across the river that sounds each time they back up. The songbirds keep speaking through it all—the whistles, pipings, prattles, buzzes, trills, stutterings, gurglings, creaks, and burbles.

And our yard catches not just the sounds but also the aromas of early summer. It's the gardenias this morning, freshly bloomed.

8:55 a.m. Driving back from breakfast, entering the neighborhood, I see one of the juvies fly off the globe of the streetlight, one of their favorite perches. The hawk stretches fully into a glide and cuts over the top of the truck. Two crows follow it. They've been waiting for some action.

30 June. 6:45 a.m. Rain all night and this morning dripping trees. I walk out onto the deck. I hear one of the juvies beside the house. The hawk is sitting about ten yards directly above me. The hawk cries—kewee, kewee, kewee, kewee. It looks down and doesn't move as I walk to the rail and answer with my own call—the whistle I've used often this year, trying to imitate the hawk's high, piercing cry. Listening closely I hear another hawk answer to the west. The two juvie birds, or possibly a juvie and an adult in the distance. I exchange four rounds of whistles with the nearby bird—setting up our own cross-species call-and-response.

I stand and stare at the hawk—knowing somehow it will stay and let me observe it. The birds are now so familiar to me, at times this year it's felt like we are closer kin than the evolutionary charts say we are; I've felt like they are acquaintances, neighbors. There are other birdsongs in the yard—cardinals and Carolina wrens up early working the feeders—but they feel a little remote.

It's now officially a week into summer. I stare at the hawk. How long will it sit there? It's a dark silhouette on the limb, a little sullen. The soaking rain's last residue drops from the limb. I take no chances. I don't narrow the gap. To do so I would have to fly.

The hawk sits comfortably above me; the hawk is interested, attentive to my presence. Sitting on the limb the juvie looks thin, almost sinewy. "Have you eaten enough?" I want to ask. "Are you learning to hunt?" I consider saying it out loud, but I stop short of speaking. I whistle again. The hawk does not answer. With no fanfare or rush, it opens its broad wings and disappears into the dripping woods.

After

Late September. It's a little cooler now. Not muggy like August. I sit and listen to the yard, a familiar soundtrack that I have not abandoned. No hawks cry though. The juvies have moved farther and farther away from the nest tree now, and I have released them in what seems a healthy cross-species uncoupling. I have almost forgotten what these hawks demanded of me day to day for a year. If our relationship was indeed commensal, then I think I got the better end of the narrative deal. The hawks still exist beyond themselves, as characters in stories I tell about the year. I'll never know if I ever was in theirs. When was the last time I checked in with them? They've been offstage for over a month. Without their calling there's a feeling of freedom in the landscape, and it extends into my own head. Or is it the other way around?

I think now that the daily form of the almanac provided cover from coming to terms with some of the serious issues of bird/human cohabitation. How close could I really get to them? Stay with it, stay engaged for one year, and it's easy to believe something has to happen. There is a payoff at the end: anything shaped into a circle (like a year) creates meaning. But after the year concluded, I thought I could just let go. I thought I had no more responsibility after late June, beyond being a human being, and that the hawks had no more purpose beyond being hawks. They could recede from my human awareness and take their place again as citizens of a much, much larger, more-than-human world. They could become almost invisible in the woods again. We could settle together back into our natural niches—human and bird, domestic and wild, dreaming wild and being wild. There could be space between our animal lives to navigate—other places, projects, and relationships could go on. I could go back to looking at the river as a thing that flows rather than watching the river for a hawk flying over the thing that flows.

Right now, though, it feels a little like a breakup. I'm sad when I don't see them on the street every day. I feel guilty not following them when I do see them. When they are absent, I feel nostalgic for the four preceding seasons, those long spiraling months of hawk-centeredness within which I was caught so deeply. I didn't anticipate this lingering bird crush. Do you know the old song "Walk away Renée?" That's how I feel. That popular song assures me that every serious relationship leaves a little residue that never goes away.

There's a noise in the flowerbed below the porch and at first I think it's a raccoon or possum. The dog is going crazy. I worry that if it's a raccoon, it's rabid. After all, why would a shy, mostly nocturnal animal be out in the lingering heat? There is no mistaking it. Something is rustling in the dull bushes just below me. It's like a stab to my heart when I catch a glimpse and see it's a skinny hawk, stumbling around.

So I fight through fear, reflection, projection, and act. I have a hawk on the ground and know that can only mean one thing: I need to help it if I can. My first hypothesis is that it has a concussion and there's been a collision with our big windows again. Maybe it's only a temporary disorientation and the bird will soon soar back into the trees. At any moment this tragedy could turn toward comedy. Maybe I should just wait it out. After all, Drew said once that hawks run into things in woods all the time. They're prepared by evolution to recover.

But I need to know, to help if I can, so I walk out of the house and into the yard. After I enter the fenced area I set up two plastic recycling containers, one on top of the other, for a makeshift crate if I need it. Then I put on my leather work gloves. I've never been close enough to a live hawk to touch it. If I get close now, I don't want to get nipped by that powerful, ripping beak.

I grab an extra jacket too, and once in the backyard, I flush the hawk from the bushes. In my panic and sadness, I think it's a red-shouldered. I remember J. A. Baker's pronouncement, that the hardest thing for us to see is what is really there. The hawk stumbles into the open, lurches left and right to get away, disoriented. I cut off its escape to the deeper yard by chasing it to the fence. The hawk cowers, both wings folded against its sides. Maybe it's been poisoned? I throw the jacket over it, pin it to the fence. I reach under and grab the hawk by its yellow legs and pull off the jacket like a magician revealing what's come out of his hat. It's the first time I've ever held a hawk in my hands. I'm surprised at how light it is. It doesn't try to bite me or fly away—just relaxes into my light grip, with huge yellow eyes, beak slightly ajar, mottled brownish breast thin and fragile. I remind myself again of a fledgling's 50 percent chance of mortality in the first year.

I carry the hawk up the hill with the jacket over it to keep it calm. I place the hawk in the makeshift container, put the other container over the top, and duct tape the two together. I carry it to the front porch. There's no struggle inside. The hawk sits silently in the dark.

I'm pretty distraught, my mind firing like fireworks and my nerves shot, so I sit down next to the crate. To fight back my feelings I think back to how I always teach Robinson Jeffers's poem "Hurt Hawks," in which the hawk with the broken wing "stands under the oak-bush and waits . . . remembers freedom / And flies in a dream." But I'm not dreaming. I'm on the edge of real panic. My hands, usually steady, are shaking a little. It's not that I didn't know an ending like this was possible. A great poem often presents us with multiple channels of feeling and experience. But I always hoped I could dodge the tragedy of the hurt hawk Jeffers embodies in his poem.

I stand up and pace. I even send a prayer to Jeffers's "wild god of the world." I listen to some sign from inside the crate, from the bird itself; I want to believe that it will fly in real air soon, not in the dream air of Jeffers's dead hawk.

I walk back inside. Finally the dog has settled down but is still on high alert. I finally call Drew and explain what's happened. "What do you think my options are?" I ask.

"If it's stunned by a window strike," Drew says, "it might recover and you can set it free. Let it stay in that dark crate overnight. See if it recovers."

Next I call a friend at the South Carolina Department of Natural Resources and ask for more advice. He gives me the name of a nearby vet that deals regularly with hurt hawks. "Take it in the morning if it's not completely recovered."

Betsy comes home and I explain that there is hurt hawk in the crate on our front porch. She looks out. The hawk sits silently inside. "Is it one of your hawks?" she asks. I tell her I think so. She sees I'm upset and tries to comfort me and assures me I'm doing the right thing. We eat dinner with the hawk outside on the front porch. Soon the darkness of the evening matches the darkness inside the crate.

That night sleep is impossible. I'm up every hour. I walk to the porch window and look out at the crate. In the yard, beyond porch, the limbs of trees form a cage of darkness around me. The only relief from the gloom are a few tiny spears of light leaking through from the streetlight. The hawk in the crate is silent and invisible. If I had a stronger imagination, I could pretend it didn't exist. But I do imagine the hawk, its heart beating in the dark. In nature it's a general rule that smaller animals like hawks have larger hearts in proportion to their body size, and they have faster heart rates. Hawks have large, four-chambered hearts and their blood travels in a figure eight through the body, just like ours. The size of a bird's heart is affected by lifestyle—flightless birds have no need for the athletic hearts of raptors. And a bird whose life is spent gliding, like the buzzards in our neighborhood last winter, need hearts with less capability than those that dive, hover, and sprint like a peregrine. A hawk's heart rate increases when it flies. Mine increases with depth of feeling—curiosity or fear, fight or flight?

I call Drew on the way to the vet to give him a status update on the hurt hawk. He asks, "How do you feel?"

"I feel a sort of frenzied sadness," I say.

"Are you sad about the hawk or is there more?" He asks.

"It's the sadness of broken things I'm feeling. It's the snake on the road, the dead crow," I say. "It's the reality of stats bearing down on all of us—actuary tables, accidents, chance, all those Darwinian probabilities."

But why be sad about the suffering of a single bird? Because you never know. Because sorrow is a way of staying alive. It's a way of seeing your own future death, or your country's death, or the death someday of a loved one in the context of now. Sadness is one of the body's ways of staying honest.

When I arrive at the vet's office I remove the crate with the quiet hawk inside. I carry the hawk straight to an examining room and the vet comes in. I explain what I know. I tell him I think it's maybe one of the young red-shouldered hawks from our yard. Maybe it's been a window strike. Maybe it's only stunned. He listens, says, "Let's take a look and see what the problem is."

He hands me a set of gloves thicker than my work gloves, like someone might use to work near a furnace. I slip them on. They're leather and so heavy I can't get the fingers to move much inside. The doctor has his own thinner pair and reaches in, grabs the bird, and hands it to me, feet first. "Hold it by the talons," he explains. I hold the hawk's legs, but as I do I see that two of the toes on one foot are badly broken, twisted sideways.

"That's not a good sign," the vet says when he sees the toes. "There was some serious trauma." My heart is beating at twice its normal rate, and it feels huge in my chest.

It's the first time since I captured the hawk against the fence that I've seen some fierceness. The hawk opens its bill and watches us both closely. Its perfectly round black pupils have tripled in size. "I'm going to test that right wing," the vet says. "Can you place your other glove between my hand and that beak?" The hawk watches as he moves the wing. The vet stretches out the wing and it functions fine. So far so good.

"Now, the other one."

I flip the hawk to its other side and the vet lifts the wing slowly. We both see it, the terrible wound. The entire joint where the wing hinges is clotted, and the white bone is sticking through the skin, a jagged, bloody, red compound fracture.

"That's a bad, bad break," he says. "This bird will never fly again, and it's very malnourished as well."

Whenever I teach the Jeffers poem, I discuss how Jeffers's sentiments about the hurt hawk are dated, and that if one was to ever have such a direct encounter with an injured bird today, we would have so many other options. We don't always have to give a hurt hawk what the poet calls "the lead gift."

But options narrow quickly with the diagnosis for this hurt hawk, and I realize the vet will soon be helping the bird "unsheath" from reality, as Robinson Jeffers describes the hawk's last moment in his poem.

The vet takes the hawk from me and I follow him to a back room. He unscrews the hinges on a small plate on the top of a plexiglass chamber, places the badly injured hawk inside, and rescrews the plate. He turns the valve on the container of gas and it hisses as it engages. The hawk struggles as the gas enters and looks directly at me as the bright yellow dulls in its eyes, the eyes close, and the life flies quickly out of it. The difference between life and death becomes obvious when you see it happen. It is a line we all cross. One side is brightly kinetic, the other, dark and still. I hold the hawk, smaller in death. The yellow toes, even the broken ones, curl inward, as if clutching an invisible branch.

I walk back out to the truck. I text Drew a picture I've taken of the dead hawk.

"Not your bird. Young Cooper's hawk," Drew texts back quickly. "Must have been chasing birds at your feeder and slammed into your wire fence. Do you feel better knowing it's not one of your birds?"

Baker's book doesn't end with death, as mine does. His ends with a sort of personal redemption. On the last page of *The Peregrine*, the watcher stands before a sleeping falcon and hopes the bird will look deep into his corrupted human soul and accept him as a fellow predator. The more the watcher stares at the falcon, the more he hopes the fierce peregrine will see beyond him and through him. I have an odd thought, remembering the last look I exchanged with the dying hawk, that as a nature writer I am what is beyond Baker's watcher. I'm fifty years in the future, and all the hawks in our yard are beyond as well. Nothing went away.

I tried to help. I did what I could once the hawk world collided with our own complex construction of our shared space, as I knew it would. There is some solace in knowing that back home the red-shouldered hawks are still hunting in the bottoms, crying out, though some wildlife biologist trying to determine a predator flow chart for our local ecology would have to factor in one less Cooper's hawk. I take the last of my notes and pull in one last shallow breath before I start the truck.

"I feel both momentary relief and deep sadness," I finally text Drew. Then add, "So this is what it meant to give my heart to the hawks."

Acknowledgments

There were a few works I kept close as I observed the neighborhood hawks, particularly a printout of Cornell University's *Birds of North America / Species Account for the Red-shouldered Hawk* authored by Scott T. Crocoll and published online initially in 2008 and revised later by Cheryl R. Dykstra and Jeffery L. Hays. Also, I found a wonderful account of red-shouldered hawks in Florida by Donald J. Nicholson that was published in the *Wilson Bulletin* in March 1930. Michael A. Godfrey's *A Sierra Club Naturalist's Guide to the Piedmont*, as always, answered landscape or natural history questions; *Sibley's Field Guide to Birds of Eastern North America* and *Peterson's Guide* were also most helpful.

For those interested in tracking down the voices that inspired this work, I became familiar with at least three editions of Baker's work: *The Peregrine* by J. A. Baker, introduction by Robert Macfarlane (NYRB Classics, 1967/2005); *The Peregrine, Hill of Summer, and Diaries* by J. A. Baker, edited by John Fanshawe, with introduction by Mark Cocker (William Collins, paperback edition 2015); and *The Peregrine* by J. A. Baker, 50th anniversary edition, with a new afterword by Robert Macfarlane (William Collins, 2017). Hetty Saunders's *My House of Sky: The Life and Work of J. A. Baker* (Little Toller Books, 2017) offers the first biography of Baker created from the first full survey of the J. A. Baker Archives. And, of course, there is Helen Macdonald's *H Is for Hawk* (Grove Press, 2014).

Drew Lanham was my lifeline—poet, ornithologist, or, as he self-describes, "wild wanderer, lover of wild edges & the uncertain dim shimmering at dawn, owner of a feral heart"; thanks, Drew, for always answering my calls; thanks to G. C. Waldrep for his poetic insight into vultures and power lines; and to Ian Marshall and all the good folks at Shaver's Creek for showing me some wild country and some birds, close up; thanks to Ann Rash for the damn good hawk story; thanks to Steve Patton for pausing with me to watch; thanks to my neighbors for tolerating my binocular-walks for a year; thanks to Savannah Paige Murray for reading the draft several times; thanks to Helen Correll for her map and to David Hale for the cover woodcut; thanks to the folks at UGA Press, Patrick Allen, Jon Davies, Erin Kirk New, and Kerrie Maynes; and finally, thank you, as always, to Betsy, who walked with me and asked about my heart.